You're Singing My Song

Keeping The Music In Your Marriage

By
GLENN AND CINDY COLLEY

You're Singing My Song

Keeping The Music In Your Marriage

Table of Contents:

Forward

It was Paul the apostle who wrote, "There hath no temptation taken you but such as is common to man... (I Cor. 10:13). Another thing common to man is struggles in marriage, and chances are good that you and your beloved have a few. This book will help. God's Word holds the key, and we have applied that key to many, many different marriage scenarios. The fact that you are reading this book says so much about you. It says that you are not satisfied with a status quo life with your partner. You don't just want a mediocre marriage, and surely not a miserable marriage. You want music in your marriage!

May we suggest you read this book with your spouse? Decide to make it a shared project for mutual enjoyment and improvement, and read a chapter every day or two, taking time over coffee for the discussion points at the end of each.

History has clearly shown that a great marriage doesn't take money, nor a high degree of education. It takes two people dedicated to God and to one another. In premarital counseling I often tell young couples that I can guarantee that their marriage will last a lifetime. If two people, compatible enough to want to marry in the first place, will never stop loving and serving God first and their mates second, the marriage won't fail. If both maintain that heart, the marriage is solid for the long haul. That's the formula.

We wrote this book together. Realizing that the material may be useful in classes of married couples, we think it's important to emphasize that the final decisions about what was included herein were always Glenn's. While we think it's important to look at most of the topics included from both a husband's and a wife's perspective (thus the inclusion of Cindy's writings), the authority in a classroom situation rests with the teacher, not with the ideas in the book. The final judgments about what is taught in any class, of course will ultimately rest with the teacher. We seek only to provide a tool, for private or group study, to facilitate learning the Will of Christ for our marriages.

We pray that hurting marriages will find healing in the pages of God's word through this study, but we hope this book will bless college groups and singles, as well. If those yet unmarried can make early decisions to do marriage God's way, the kingdom of God will be fortified by faithful and secure families. Preventing pain is far better than treating it.

Enjoy the book. May it put a little music in your marriage!

Dedication

This book is dedicated to our parents Gary and Maggie Colley, and Lee and Johnnia Holder, whose combined 90 years of marriage taught us how to make love work for a lifetime.

Unless otherwise noted, Scripture references are from the New King James translation of the Bible.

CHAPTER ONE

Leave and Cleave

About Leaving

Bo and Ashley marry right out of high school. Because they are so young, and Ashley's mom and dad have a finished basement complete with bedroom and bath, they'll live there rent-free for a while. They'll just eat their meals upstairs with the folks. Ashley has always been close to her folks, and her dad feels good that he can help them out and make sure Ashley is safe. After all, she'll always be his little girl. And the house has plenty of evidence to prove it. The hallway upstairs is lined with stairstep pictures starting twenty years ago, then to the little girl shots, then to braces and poofy hair, then to high school, and when she started dating Bo. She grew up here and it feels good to be home—and to have her new husband Bo.

In this chapter we want to take a look at a principle so important in finding the music in marriage that it is repeated three different times in the Bible, both in the Old and New Testaments: Leave and cleave.

> *"Therefore a man shall leave his father and mother and be joined to his wife, and they shall become one flesh"* (Genesis 2:24).

> **"Have you not read that He who made *them* at the beginning made them male and female and said, 'For this reason a man shall leave his father and mother and be joined to his wife, and the two shall become one flesh'?"** (Matt. 19:4-5).

> *"For this reason a man shall leave his father and mother and be joined to his wife, and the two shall become one flesh"* (Ephesians 5:31).

I know that families are different, and I know that there are special circumstances which require young couples to live in arrangements which tie them closely to their parents. I further know that the Bible doesn't specify how far one must be from his parents to "leave" and "cleave". But one more thing I know: Many marriages never get a fighting chance because parents and child haven't been brave enough to figure this one out.

There are three different parties who must know their roles in this arrangement called marriage: husband, wife, and parents.

The Parents

As far as I know, no parent of grown children ever considered himself or herself to be interfering; not even the mother I knew who refused to speak to her daughter a few weeks before the wedding until the girl would relent to do the wedding the way the mother wanted. We parents aren't born understanding this matter of letting go. In our minds it is never interfering or disobeying God. We are simply helping; that's all. "I'm successful in business. I've got the wherewithal to do it. Why should I wait until I die to give them the money? Besides, no son of mine is going to live in the kind of shack his salary would pay for. How would that look?! They are newlyweds now and could really use it."

When I was in fourth grade our teacher, Mrs. Holmes (the most beautiful woman in the world whom I fully intended to marry), got us some fertilized eggs and an incubator, and we learned about baby chicks. We maintained the temperature and exercised caution to do just what Mrs. Holmes told us. We couldn't wait. One day there was a tiny hole being pecked out of one of the eggs, then the same happened with another. Do you know what every student in that fourth grade class was inclined to do? Of course you do. We wanted to help that infant chick out. We were bigger, stronger, and loved them. Why should we have to go through the stress of watching them strain, stretch and wiggle their way out when we could do this easily for them?

There's something in a young couple marrying that's like that. I'm not sure I knew the value of what Cindy and I were going through back then in our first few years of marriage. Sometimes it was tough. I bought our furniture from yard sales, and refinished it in the yard. Someone gave us a refrigerator, and I sanded the rust off and spray painted it. If you put the milk in the very back it wouldn't spoil. The night after we signed that paper for that little frame house, Cindy and I sat in my Cutlass in the driveway and I held her as she cried. I had a job, but were we doing the right thing to obligate ourselves for more money than ever before in our lives? $175 a month doesn't grow on trees you know.

We shopped for groceries together because it represented a large expenditure and we thought we'd prefer doing it side by side. Cindy naturally made almost all the choices, but I was there for her.

Both sets of parents could have afforded to do many of those things for us, and they certainly did help us. For a wedding present my folks bought us a mattress and gave us the down payment for the house. Cindy's parents gave us a table and chairs for the kitchen. But they both understood the point of this chapter. That was our house, and those were our groceries, and this was our marriage. The two of us made a family. It was sometimes hard, but it felt good.

There are genuine emergencies, and I'm not saying we should take this principle to a ridiculous extreme. But a wise father and mother know the difference between the healthy struggle of new-lyweds to make it on their own, and an emergency.

The Young Wife

I counseled and married a couple a few years ago who were on the verge of receiving a lot of money. Her father was well off, and had created a trust years ago which put the money in her possession when she turned twenty-five. I mean a lot of money. Her private concern to me was this: Do I tell my fiancé? If I don't, it seems I'm not being completely honest with him. If I do tell him, how will that affect his sense of duty to work hard and provide for us in these early years? Will we be tempted to overextend credit, knowing the windfall is just around the corner? Good questions. She did tell him, and I had them sign a private agreement between them on their wedding day which vowed in every way I could think of that they would work and live and love, as much as was in them, as if that money didn't exist.   Would you say that upcoming money was a blessing or a curse?

Naturally parental interference doesn't just come in the form of money. Just as often it comes in the form of dominance. Imagine a twenty-three year old husband coming in from work to hear his wife on the phone in the next room. "Yes, Mama, we argued for over an hour!...Yes!...And do you know what he said after that?...He did too say it!...If he thinks he's getting close to me tonight, he's got another think coming..." How does that young husband feel? Terrible. Terrible because he argued with his wife, terrible because she seems to him to care more about her mother than about him, and terrible because he thought those kinds of matters were private—just between him and his wife. It isn't wrong for a wife to seek advice from her wise mother or father. But it is wrong for her to make her husband feel the way that husband feels right now. She doesn't belong to her parents any more. She left them and took this man's name. She is his.

I'd rather a young wife didn't say to her husband, "I'd like to go home this weekend,"
referring to her parents house. She should say, "I'd like to go see my parents this weekend." You see, her home isn't with them anymore. Her home is wherever her beloved husband is.

The Young Husband

Young couples should love their parents, and what Paul said in Ephesians 6:1-4 about honoring your parents is true for your lifetime.   How do you know the difference between healthy inter-action and unhealthy interference? Here is the warning light: when one or the other spouse feels that the in-laws are interfering. Is it true? If it is, the spouse whose parents are causing the prob-lem should address it first and do so gently. Just a well-timed kind word to say we need more space for us will usually do the trick. If it is not well received and does not accomplish the pur-pose, it is the husband's role to find the solution regardless of whose parents are the trouble.

Some husbands and wives and their parents get along fine in the same town. The grandparents are helpful as babysitters when needed. But this only works well if everyone knows his role and doesn't cross the lines which govern and show respect for each

mily. We have good friends in Virginia who do this well. Cal
a d Pat have two grown daughters, both of whom have grown
c ildren now, and both of whom have lived all their married lives

in the same city as their parents. They spend time together and always have. But they know the secret of leaving and cleaving, and that's how they keep the music in their marriages.

About Cleaving

Enough about the leaving part. What about the cleaving part? The original Greek word in Matthew nineteen, verse five is all about adherence. It literally denotes a gluing together forming a bond of the firmest kind.

Have you ever joined two pieces of wood together with carpenter's glue and clamps? If it is done right, the glued joint becomes stronger than either piece of wood by itself. This is particularly true when the pieces joined are dove-tailed or lap-jointed together, each fitting its idiosyncrasies in the perfect space left void by the other. The idea is that if you ever want to get those two pieces of wood apart again, you are going to have to break one of them off at a point other than the joint. Each piece of wood is "committed" at the point of that joining once that glue has dried.

Marriage is an adventure. It's a journey. It's a mystery and your own personal edition of non-fictional romance. But successful marriage must be, above all, a commitment.

Have you applied the great Carpenter's glue to your marriage? "Unless the Lord builds the house, they labor in vain that build it," (Psalm 127:1). Marriage is an adventure. It's a journey. It's a mystery and your own personal edition of non-fictional romance. But successful marriage must be, above all, a commitment. Sometimes the adventure will lapse into boredom, the journey into retreat, the mystery into routine and the romance into disappointment. What about these times?

The answer is agape love. Agape is the committed kind of love. Unfettered by circumstances and unrealized expectations, it is the Carpenter's glue. It is what demands that one or the other of us will have to be destroyed if we are ever to be severed. We're simply not coming unglued.

All it takes is two completely committed hearts. It doesn't

depend on the confidence your parents have about your union (although their premarital counsel is often very valuable). Friends who are encouraging or discouraging your union will likely soon fade from your sphere of influence. It just takes two completely committed hearts. But it does take two completely committed hearts to be the best marriage it can be. Once you say, "I do," you die to self and become alive to your spouse. Through the years, it won't be your love that sustains your marriage; it will be your marriage that sustains your love. This is life-long commitment.

We often tell young Christians who are contemplating marriage to picture her in sixty-five years, aged, sitting in the dining room at the nursing home. Picture him bald and having removed his dentures before crawling into bed with you. Picture her with flabby arms and picture him with toenail fungus. It can (and likely will) happen! Can you still love him? Is she still attractive to you? If so, you have a good start on full-blown agape love.

When talking to people whose marriages are in trouble, we always ask each partner individually, "Are you willing to do whatever it takes to save this marriage? There is little chance of salvaging that home if either partner answers no. Can you both sign the following pledge? If the answer is no, and you can't be led to such a commitment, get another book-- maybe one on how to survive a suffering marriage, or maybe even how to get through a divorce. And get a big box of Kleenex to go with it. There is a lot of sorrow headed your way.

As I begin this study, I pledge to do all I can do to make our marriage the best it can be. I understand that marriage is a lifetime commitment, and I am willing to make whatever sacrifices I am called upon to make for the good of our union.

Signed: _____ *(Husband)*

_____ *(Wife)*

Date: _____

Think About It:

1. Can you think of Bible examples of interference in marriages (Laban, Jezebel, etc.)?

2. One daughter-in-law said her parents-in-law came over unexpectedly a couple of times a week. Her husband felt obligated to welcome them in whether or not he and his wife had plans to relax, be intimate, have a quiet dinner alone, watch an old black and white movie together, etc. He was afraid of hurting their feelings. What should he have done?

3. What action would be appropriate for a young couple when they first realize they have a problem with parental interference? What if they are indebted to those parents?

4. Discuss the balance between caring for elderly parents and marital independence.

5. List areas of common vulnerability with parental relationships (such as child discipline, money, career choices, etc.).

When Life's Changes Come

When the crimson leaves have fallen
And cool winds breathe a sigh,
I stop beneath a barren oak
And wistfully think, "Why?"

Why must flowers lose their blooms?
Where goes the butterfly?
Why does autumn bear this chill?
Where do the birds go and why?

The squirrels don't forget to find acorns.
The fields never fail to turn gold.
The mice find my barn for the winter,
And I've turned another year old.

Every appointment of nature
Is met with the greatest detail.
How can all heaven and earth do His will
And I, in His own image, fail?

If I could, like stars in their courses,
Or that gold harvest moon in the night,
Follow the course He has charted
And change when He thought it was right;

If I had no fear of tomorrow;
If I trusted in God's wisdom more,
Like the squirrel I'd be ready for winter;
Like the bird flying south, I could soar.

The heavens and earth shout His glory.
The sky is the work of His hand
I, too, have a place in my God's world.
I, too, must attend His command.

Seedtime and harvest, death before life;
In His good time may I take my place
As the whole world gives way and all nature obeys,
In the seasons, may I see His face.

Cindy Colley

CHAPTER TWO

Singing Solomon's Song

Communication is the Key

Single people may not understand this, but after 28 years of marriage, not only have Cindy and I not run out of things to say to each other, but I am simply addicted to talking to her. When our work involves traveling separately, we are determined to phone at least once every day even when we are on opposite sides of the planet! But this chapter is not merely about the joy of communication with your spouse, but the importance of it. Plainly put, you will communicate or your marriage will disintegrate.

I don't remember hearing many sermons on the Song of Solomon. Occasionally a writer will assert that these pages, filled with words of love between Solomon and his Shulamite wife, must be a metaphor for Christ and His church, and that such is the Holy Spirit's point in giving it to us. Such is speculative and I have never seen convincing evidence. It is much simpler to view the Song of Solomon at face value and take it for what it is: an intimate example of communication between a man and his young wife.

According to Dr. Richard G. Moulton's Modern Reader's Bible, (as quoted from J. Sidlow Baxter's book, *Explore the Book*), the Song of Solomon is "A suite of Seven Idyls." These, the titles of which we have reworded somewhat, are as follows:

Idyle 1. The Royal Wedding Lived Over Again (1:1 – 2:7).
Idyle 2. The Bride's Courtship Reminiscences (2:8 – 3:5).
Idyle 3. The Occasion of the Betrothal Recalled (3:6 – 5:1).
Idyle 4. The Bride's Troubled Dream Related (5:2 – 6:3).
Idyle 5. The King's Meditation on His Bride (6:4 – 7:10).
Idyle 6. The Bride Longs to See Her Old Home (7:11 – 8:4).
Idyle 7. The Renewal of Love at Lebanon (8:5 – 8:14).

This is a beautiful love poem that has had a way of weaving its music into the hearts of husbands and wives who want to learn the secret of healthy communication in marriage. The bread and water of great marriage is communication. Without it you will never enjoy your marriage as fully as God planned for you to do. It's no accident that after Peter revealed seven truth-filled verses about husbands and wives in I Peter 3, he says, "For he that will love life, and see good days, let him refrain his tongue from evil, and his lips that they speak no guile" (I Pet. 3:10). How many marriages do you know right now which are in crisis largely because husbands and wives haven't been dedicated enough to communicating and doing so in a healthy way?

I'm unsure of the origin of this alliteration, but our different levels of communication can be classified in five levels: the frivolous level, the factual level, the fellowship level, the feeling level, and the freedom level. Let's take them one at the time.

The frivolous level is one used in brief conversations with store clerks and people waiting on an elevator beside you. It is a friendly and courteous, "Good morning, I hope you are doing well," which we in the South usually abbreviate to "Morning," with a brief nod of the head. This level is an uncomplicated, but important lubricant in the daily machine of human nature. Casual, friendly interaction.

Second, the factual level. This is the one we practice with a secretary when giving her instructions or a gas station attendant when getting directions. Like a news commentary, it is perhaps (should be) pleasant, but it is primarily to get to the facts. This level has no emotional attachment.

Third, the fellowship level. This often initiates friendship. On this level we begin to risk a little because as we sit at that church social or that club meeting, we begin expressing our ideas, judgments, and philosophies. When you do that, you enjoy the conversation more, but you also start risking rejection. The person listening to you could potentially respond negatively to your thoughts.

Fourth, the feeling level. The feeling level takes us even farther and makes us even more vulnerable to rejection. At this level I express not only my judgments, but how I actually feel about these things. This level exposes more of a man's heart. Most of us don't communicate at this level before we really believe we can trust the other person. This level, frankly, is the highest level of communication many people ever experience. That's sad, because the next level is where the greatest joy in marriage it to be found.

Finally, the freedom level of communication. This one, existing especially for marriage, is one in which I can feel free to speak openly with my spouse. I can talk of my hopes and dreams, frustrations and pains, while trusting that my husband or wife loves me and will treat these innermost thoughts with kindness, respect, and privacy. That doesn't mean that she won't express herself too, even to disagree, but she will never express contempt or mockery for this from-the-heart communication.

The word "*intimacy*" comes from a Latin word meaning inmost. This intimate, freedom level of communication involves things you would share with no one on earth except the one with whom you are most intimate. This is the most satisfying level of communication, and many never find it. With your spouse you should grow to the point at which you can speak freely of your dreams, fears, secrets, failures, and aspirations. It is interesting that when the sexual intimacy of marriage is mentioned in the Scriptures it is sometimes phrased "a man knew his wife" (see Lk. 1:34). That's the idea of intimacy. Intimacy in marriage which is only physical is crippled and weak. It is void and without much meaning. God has given us the tools in His word for true intimacy. Physical, emotional, and spiritual intimacy with your spouse means "dwelling with her according to knowledge" (I Pet. 3:7).

Now, what can we learn about communication in marriage from the Song of Solomon?

They talk a lot. Around sixty percent of this book consists of words between Solomon and his Shulamite wife (Song 6). When they are separated they miss the sound of one another's voices. They need each other's company and they praise each others speech. Either husband or wife is free to speak without embarrassment.   The other is free to receive the words without resentment.

We need to learn to talk to each other. Who would you say has the most trouble with this facet of your marriage? Often it's the husband. Many of us just don't have the same instinctive drive to sit and talk with our wives every day as they do with us. The reasons are many. One is that we husbands tend to be goal oriented. Our wives naturally assumed that the same massive quantity of conversation which characterized us when we dated would hold true after we were married.   In the summer after we had dated a year in college, I wrote Cindy a letter every day–and that wasn't email, either.   I'd get home from my job as a carpenter's gopher ("go-for-this" and "go-for-that") worn out in the evenings, but I'd always find the energy before bed to write to the one I loved and walk the letter out to the mail box. When we talked on the phone that summer, we spent most of the time talking about when we could see each other and talk some more. I hate to admit it, but more than once in our marriage Cindy has referenced those times and reminded me that I've slipped a little. Men try harder before they are married because, as unromantic as it sounds, they are pursuing a goal: marrying the girl they adore. Yet, having achieved marriage, an unwise husband may leave that communication and simply pursue his next goal.

Consider also that we have background differences. We weren't raised to show our emotions. We seldom cry, and we don't ask directions when we can't find the way on our maps. Perhaps for some of us the problem with being good communicators with our wives is that such seems to threaten our feelings of self-reliance. We need our wives to view us as heroes, and silence helps show we are in control of our immediate world.

And frankly, sometimes the communication suffers simply because we are too busy. Just remember Sir, that while God expects you to work and support your family (I Tim. 5:8), your job is the means toward that end.   It is not the end in itself. It is the means by which you make the money to enjoy and care for your family. Men who neglect their wives and children because they enjoy the thrill of working and earning money are making a mistake which will surface later in their lives in the form of regret. In his book *What Wives Wish Their Husbands Knew about Women*, James Dobson writes of one husband who made a talking chair in their bedroom. Every night, no matter how tired he was, he sat there and gave her talk-time in which he completely focused on her. He looked her in the eyes, and responded to what she said appropriately. It's a great idea, and his wife loved it (1975, pp.12,13).

Observe something else. Solomon and his wife have nicknames for one another. He calls her his dove.

I sleep, but my heart is awake; It is the voice of my beloved! He knocks, saying, "Open for me, my sister, *my love,* my dove, my perfect one; For my head is covered with dew, my locks with the drops of the night" (Song 5:2, emphasis added).

Pet names between spouses are personal. They may make others smile or wink, but they have a way of making spouses feel special. Do you have a pet name for your wife; a name that belongs exclusively to her?

It is reciprocal. See the verse again and notice that she calls him her "beloved". Cindy and I know a wonderful Christian couple who frequently call each other affectionate names in front of us and talk in silly, affectionate ways to each other. To hear her talk you'd think he was the greatest husband alive with no close second! While some husbands would chuckle and blush a little when their wives showed such verbal affection around others, most would love it. And when wives hear these affectionate nicknames they know it is a sweet way for their husbands to say, "You are special to me. I love you because of your unique characteristics. I'm loving the fact that we are living our lives together." Peter wrote "Wives, submit yourselves unto your own husbands...." The Greek word for *own* in that verse is *idios* (id'-ee-os), the word from which we get our English word idiosyncrasy. In other words, Peter urges that a wife is to be in submission to her unique husband, one who is different from all others. Both husbands and wives need to feel they are unique in the eyes of their mates.

The freedom level of speech, which should be the goal of every husband or wife reading this book, can only be achieved in an atmosphere of acceptance.

Solomon also teaches us that in marriage our words should be positive. Sir, do you make an effort every day to affirm your wife and maintain her self-esteem? The Good Book says we are to love our wives as our own bodies, and that a man who loves his wife loves himself (Eph. 5). Do yourself a favor and practice speaking positively to that sweet woman whom God gave you, and listen again to our young king:

I sleep, but my heart is awake; It is the voice of my beloved! He knocks, saying, "Open for me, my sister, my love, my dove, my perfect one; For my head is covered with dew, my locks with the drops of the night.

Key in on the word *perfect*.

This Hebrew word, *tam* {tawm}, is defined by Strong's Lexicon this way: "Complete, perfect. One who lacks nothing in physical strength, beauty, etc..." Now, I am sure she was a beautiful woman with many admirable characteristics, but *perfect*? We all know no one is perfect. How do you explain this sort of description from her husband? Simple. He is affirming her, building her up. We all have known men who practice the opposite and speak in a critical way to their wives, even in front of others. They are hurting themselves. But a man who compliments his wife this way makes her feel wanted, needed, and special. Look at two other verses and see how Solomon does this.

I have compared you, my love, To my filly among Pharaoh's chariots. Your cheeks are lovely with ornaments, Your neck with chains of gold. We will make you ornaments of gold With studs of silver.
(Song 1:9-11)

Behold, you are fair, my love! Behold, you are fair! You have dove's eyes.
Behold, you are handsome, my beloved! Yes, pleasant! Also our bed is green. The beams of our houses are cedar, And our rafters of fir.
(Song 1:15-17).

Paul wrote, "Let your speech be always with grace, seasoned with salt, that you may know how you ought to answer every man" (Col. 4:6). Grace and salt. Salt is what adds flavor to food and makes it a pleasure to eat. Our speech should include the kind of words which make what we are saying as pleasant as possible. Grace is unmerited favor. It isn't giving someone what he deserves, but what he needs. Applied to our speech, it means saying that which builds people up and encourages them. It isn't lying to say to your husband, "You are the best looking husband (or most thoughtful, or most intelligent, etc...) in the whole state." I suppose he already knows that he isn't, but hearing you say such things has a wonderful way of making him feel appreciated. He wants so much to be admired in your eyes.

Why is it so important to affirm your spouse with positive words? Because the freedom level of speech, which should be the goal of every husband or wife reading this book, can only be achieved in an atmosphere of acceptance. If a wife is constantly critical, seldom or never complimentary, always looking for her husband's faults, he cannot open up and speak freely around her. Oh, they will talk, but he will become very good at hiding his inner feelings for fear of rebuttal. He will wear a sort of communication mask showing her only the parts of his heart he feels safe showing her and she'll never see the rest of him. The only way husbands and wives can enjoy healthy communication and musical marriage is if both practice being positive. That doesn't mean we don't deal with problems responsibly and work through struggles; it simply means we think every day about making our marriage partners happy and confident. "His mouth is most sweet: yea, he is altogether lovely. This is my beloved, and this is my friend..."(Song 5:16).

We need to work on this level of intimacy in our marriages because of the amazing freedom and love it creates. You never arrive at perfection, but you need to make a start if you want to have a happy home.

Think about it:
1. Why is the freedom level of communication a worthwhile goal in marriage?

2. Why is it so important for your wife to know you speak openly with her?

3. What does your spouse do that makes the freedom level of conversation easy or difficult for you?

4. How could a wife tell her husband that she wants the freedom level of communication, while at the same time inhibiting it?

5. What things could you do that your husband would see as affirming? What about your wife?

6. Does the freedom level of communication mean that I always

speak my mind to my mate regardless of what I'm thinking? Why or why not?

7. Research gender communication. How many words do women speak each day, on the average? What about men?

8. Find passages that emphasize the importance of listening in relationships.

Sometimes at the End of a Very Hard Day...

I don't need your brain to strategize and find a good solution.
I don't need your lips to utter forth your manly elocution.
I don't need your eyes to give me that "I could have told you" glare.
Or your hand across your mouth agape that says "You didn't dare!"

Sometimes...

All I need is your shoulder, your ears to hear my distresses.
Your arms to reach out and hold me while I tell you about the day's messes;
Your voice, when I randomly pour out my soul, to say, "Well, I understand,"
Your eyes to look into mine and the gentle caress of your hand.

Sometimes...

I don't need you to fix it for me. I'm not into your shop for repairs.
I'm still okay at this mothering job. I just need somebody who cares.
I just want to talk to someone over six...somebody without ADD.
Somebody who thinks I'm a competent girl; just someone to listen to me.

Cindy Colley

Works Cited:

Dobson, James C. (1975) *What Wives Wish Their Husbands Knew about Women* (Wheaton, IL, Tyndale Publishing)
Baxter, J. Sidlow (1960) *Explore the Book* (Grand Rapids, MI, Zondervan Publishing)

CHAPTER THREE

Being A Superhero

Marriage to Cindy is an adventure. Someone once told me that while dating you learn fifty percent of a woman, and then you spend the remainder of your life learning the other fifty percent. I must say however, that I've learned a good bit of that last fifty from God's word. Dr. Harley wrote the now benchmark book, *"His Needs Her Needs"* in which he listed the five most basic needs of women and five most basic needs of men.

Women's Needs
1. Affection
2. Conversation
3. Honesty and openness
4. Financial support
5. Family commitment

Men's Needs
1. Sexual fulfillment
2. Recreational companionship
3. An attractive spouse
4. Domestic support
5. Admiration (1997, pp.12,13)

If you are thinking now of your own spouse and of yourself, you may not consider these lists perfectly accurate, but close. That's interesting to me, but not as interesting as the fact that Harley's findings sort of mirror what the Bible says on the subject. Have you considered the last verse of Ephesians five? The latter part of this chapter is so relevant to getting marriage right that no book on the subject is really complete without it. Let's focus on the very last verse now:

"Nevertheless let every one of you in particular so love his wife even as himself; and the wife *see* that she reverence *her* husband" (Eph. 5:33).

What Paul, by inspiration, has done is encapsulate the whole matter of what a husband needs from his wife and what she needs from her man. It's the summation of all Paul has just written, and it needs to be emblazoned on the heart of every husband and wife.

She needs him to love her as he loves himself.

It isn't wrong to love yourself in a healthy way. It's *healthy*. These kinds of commands would make no sense if it was wrong to love self. Jesus taught man to love his neighbor the same way, "as himself" (Mk. 12:33). Loving someone as yourself is unceasing, solid, dependable, protecting (reasonable people never hurt themselves deliberately), and imaginative. (Don't you imagine what you should wear to look your best, and what you can do to take care of your body, etc.?)

One specific of loving her this way is described in I Peter 3:7: "Likewise, ye husbands, dwell with *them* according to knowledge, giving honor unto the wife, as unto the weaker vessel, and as being heirs together of the grace of life; that your prayers be not hindered." The ESV says, "...live with your wives in an understanding way...."

The problem many Christian husbands have isn't with loving their wives enough, but with communicating that love to their wives. The first question many husbands, by implication, are asking with their lack of romance is "Why bother? We are as married as we can be. We love each other. She understands me and I understand her. I just don't think much about romance anymore. That's something we did when we were teenagers, but we've outgrown that."

I couldn't disagree more. With such a disposition you may very well stay married, but this chapter is about getting from marriage everything good the Lord intended us to have. Ephesians 5:33 says we are to love our wives as ourselves. How do I express that to my wife?

The word romance isn't in the Scriptures, but the concept certainly is. When Peter said "Dwell with them according to knowledge..." he implied that women are different from men and that husbands need to find what makes their wives tick. A husband who either doesn't care about what her needs are, or who doesn't bother to meet them isn't obeying that command.   I expect her to meet my needs; I should seek to meet hers.   It's interesting that God sees some acts of affection to be natural (Romans 1:26, 27). Yet to husbands He says, "You've got to get knowledge on this."

Come to this reality, Sir: All wives who read this book have something in common. They like their husbands to express affection and affirm love by doing romantic things. Your wife didn't just wake up and decide one day to be this way or have this need. I suppose all women have it; thus it is instinctive. God made women with this need. Your wife didn't just decide to be like that, anymore than one day you, Sir, decided to need sex on a regular basis.

The dictionary lists ten different definitions for romance. We are speaking specifically in this chapter of those actions by a husband which communicate to his wife validation, security, reassurance, and value. Ephesians 5: 29 says, "For no man ever yet hated his own flesh; but nourishes and cherishes it, even as the Lord the church." *Cherishes* in the original Greek language means to *warm with body heat*. The previous verse says, "So ought men to love their wives as their own bodies. He that loves his wife loves himself."

Big secret here: A man who takes care of his wife is being good to himself. He takes care of her and it somehow translates into benefiting him. While each mate is to do the right things with the right attitudes to please God, it is also true that it is ten times easier to do your part if your spouse is interested in pleasing you. A man whose wife is strongly aware and supportive of his sexual needs will naturally find it easier to be romantic toward her. A woman whose husband is always thinking of new ways to be romantic will find it easier to be his close friend in the bedroom. "Love her as your own body." Failure to care for your body is physical suicide. Failure to take care of your wife is matrimonial suicide.

Does your wife need your romantic attention? That question reminds me of a traveling salesman who rang the bell and waited. A boy who couldn't have been over 10 answered, smoking the biggest cigar the salesman had ever seen. After a few seconds of stunned silence the salesman finally asked, "Is your mom home?" The boy said, "What do you think?"

This is obvious! Your wife needs what we are discussing today. If you wonder if I'm right, and she is sitting beside you, look at her right now, ask her, and see if her head begins bobbing up and down enthusiastically.

Here are things a husband needs to remember about romancing his wife. First, remember how a woman keeps score.

A man thinks he scores high with his wife when he does something very big for her, like buying her a diamond ring or taking her on a vacation she's needing. He assumes he scores less when he does something romantic but small, such as opening her car door, buying her flowers, or writing a note to tell her he's thinking of her during the day. This is yet another example of men and women assuming that if our mates love us they will show it and react to it as we do. But we are different. When a woman keeps score, no matter how big or small a gift of love is, it scores one point. Each gift has pretty much the same value. When they argue and she blurts out "you never do anything romantic any more!" he may object, "What are you talking about? Just last anniversary I bought you that ring and took you to Ruth's Chris Steak House." He thought he got 50 points for that because it cost so much. Nope. Just one. Understand this: Just as a woman may fulfill her husband's sexual needs and thinks, "Well, that ought to do it," he needs her again pretty soon. A woman's desire for "romance" is tied to a NEED. She needs constant affirmation of your love to feel secure. She loves it. She thrives on it. It energizes her. And the need is a daily one.

Finally, if you want to impress your wife with that romantic gesture, think of it all by yourself. Creativity shows you think of her and of how to please her. Such shows forethought. Forethought from a husband is translated L-O-V-E. She sees that she is blessed to have a husband who is thinking of her.

The five great categories of showing your wife you love her:

O.K., here is the list. We have given some thought to this and believe this to be the complete, exhaustive list of major categories of romancing your wives. (If you think of another, email it to us quick.)

1. The "Cary Grant" category.

This man is sentimental. He does things which say, "I'm wild about you woman." Sneak into her bathroom while she showers with a towel you heated in the dryer. Write her mushy, playful e-mails. Mail some notes to her. I once took a post-it pad and wrote a series of individual hints for a treasure hunt for Cindy to go all over the house looking for a present I had gotten for her. She loved it.   Spend a few days making a secret list of 100 things you love and appreciate about her. Take her out to eat in the evening and give it to her. Bring Kleenex. Unless there are serious on-going problems, she will love you for this. Keep a mental note when she says she admires something she saw at the store. If you can afford it, secretly buy it for a special gift. (Wrap all presents. Women love to unwrap presents). If you want more ideas I suggest a book entitled *The RoMANtic's Guide* (2000).

Big secret here: A man who takes care of his wife is being good to himself.

2. The "Mr. Clean" category.

This man does things that are helpful and lift her load. Sometimes a sweet wife is working hard in the kitchen or on laundry while her husband is reclining in the Lazy Boy. While this isn't always wrong, you need to show her you care about helping her. In our marriage/family seminars we will often ask women to write the most romantic thing their husbands have done for them over the last two weeks. Now, if you asked the husbands the same question, the answers would often and naturally lean toward the sexual. But the wives will almost never say anything sexual. They speak of helping her with housework and with children. There's something for us to figure out here gentlemen. Women love husbands who ease their work burden.

When we are about to have company my wife always likes to have the house in good shape. I really appreciate that about her. She takes pride in our home and the house she oversees. While this isn't all I do to try and help her, at those crunch times I like to say, "Honey, I've got an hour to spare here. You can have it. What would you like me to do? Give me the hard stuff." She gives me things that to her seem more difficult ("Will you do the bathrooms?"), but since I don't do them every week, they aren't a chore at all for me.

3. The "Santa Claus" category.

Never forget the special days.   Christmas is easy. I'm talking about anniversary, her birthday, Mother's Day. Again, remember that the key is that you are thinking of her and want to please her. She will really love it if you surprise her one day for a "special occasion" that she can't remember. Smile and tell her this is the anniversary of your first date, or of the first time she held your hand, or of the first time you started believing she loved you. She will want to know if you're for real about knowing the exact date of that last one. Assure her that you are certain.

Cindy and I have some good friends who furnish a horror story for men on this subject. Early on the day of her birthday (which he had totally forgotten) he found the Christmas card he had put under his truck seat last December and forgotten. Finding this amusing, he walked in the house, handed it to her and said, "Merry Christmas." She assumed he was joking and she was opening a birthday card. Nope. A Christmas card. She still didn't tell him. On the way home from Wednesday night Bible study that evening he stopped by Wal-Mart and bought himself a new tackle box. Putting it into the car he said, "Well I just bought myself a birthday present."

She paused, looked at him and said, "It isn't your birthday, Honey. It's mine." Needless to say, this day was long remembered.

Write important dates on your calendar at the beginning of each year. Remembering or forgetting these dates will make equally profound impressions on your wife. Make sure the impressions are positive.

4. The "Michael Bolton" Category.

Michael is an artist who sang "When a Man Loves a Woman", and for that song his name heads this important category.

This one is simple: When a wise husband is in front of others, he never criticizes his wife about anything; not even if he's joking. He finds things to compliment about her: cooking, creativity, child rearing, soul-winning, the way she wears her hair...whatever.   Just because a subject arises which makes him think of his wife and how another man's wife is better at this than his, he will never verbalize it. Haven't you ever cringed at hearing a husband say, "These biscuits are wonderful-soft and fluffy! You could use my wife's biscuits to brick a sidewalk!" She might chuckle, but she is embarrassed. A wise man will never do that. Prudence makes him hold his tongue. Furthermore, he knows that if his wife is like most women, a genuine compliment from him about his wife in front of others will mean she takes his hand and squeezes it lovingly when they are leaving that conversation with their friends.

Never pass up an opportunity to compliment your wife in front of others. If you have something to criticize about her, wait until you are very alone. Even then, be sure you want to say it.

By the way, this one works just as well in the way a wife speaks of her husband in front of others.

5. The "Superman" Category.

Here's the man who gets his wife out of her fix without grumping. One day she calls him at work and she has locked herself out of the house or car. Now sir, you have two choices but only one outcome. The outcome is you are surely going to help her out of this problem. You can either become frustrated and say, "I can't believe you did that. I am so covered up right now and this is the last thing I need." Now, imagine how that course of action will turn out. Hurt feelings. She'll remember that statement when you want her to be close to you that night and she will not feel very close to you. The other choice is to think before you speak and then say, "Honey, don't worry. I'll be right there." When you get there she will naturally be apologizing for her mistake, and she'll be sorry for interrupting your work day. You respond, "Oh, that's okay, baby, I've done it before myself and I'm sure I'll do it again. Say lady, you look good—you want to take fifteen minutes with me for a cup of coffee?" That's Superman.

She wants to rearrange the living room furniture. You know, it's pretty nice when she needs the strong arms of her man. Smile and say, "Here, let me get that for you, it's heavy."

I know of a wife whose husband had a two-wheel trailer hooked up to the family SUV which he had driven to his office one day. His wife came in their other car, needing the SUV for an errand. He said he was happy to swap vehicles with her but "Backing a trailer is challenging—you want me to back it out for you?" Her mood already wasn't too good and she insisted she could do it. Although she had never backed a two-wheel trailer she reasoned it couldn't be too difficult. "Just keep the steering wheel straight and the trailer will back straight." Immediately that little trailer jack-knifed and punctured the side of that SUV as her husband watched from the office door. Again, sir, you have two choices that share the same outcome. The outcome is that you will have to pay to fix the vehicle. The choice is how you will treat her. The Superman will take a deep breath, overcome his stinging frustration, and say, "Well, it's not too bad. At least you're not hurt. Those things are mighty hard to back. I did that myself one time. I can have it fixed. It's O.K." She will see you as a man unlike any other.

Think about it:

1. Why does romance mean dramatically different things to husbands and their wives?

2. Which of these five romance categories is most pleasing to your wife? Why?

3. Husbands, go down the list of five. Where are you strong? Where are you weak? Have you done all five in the last seven days?

4. Go through Dr. Harley's lists of man's and woman's greatest needs. Number them in order according to how important each thing is to you and show it to your spouse. Find a   quiet time to discuss these, taking turns just listening.

5. In which of the five hero categories does your husband excel? Tell him.

My Superman

He doesn't have a long red cape
Or a fear of Kryptonite.
He can't stop a locomotive
Or set a falling building right.

But when he dons that big red towel
And flies down the nursery hall,
When he coaches my personal favorite team:
The Rascals in pee-wee T-ball;

When he bursts through the door with a rose in his mouth
And Chinese take-out in his hands;
When he vacuums the den after game night
Or winks at me up in the stands;

When he rescues me bravely from laundry
Or just gently reaches out for my hand;
When he kneels at our bedside and talks to His God,
In these times, he's my Superman!

Cindy Colley

27 Unique Ideas for Dates
By Jeff Cohen

Planning a great date will score you major relationship points. The key is to understand your personal style and preferences as well as those of your date. Here are some unique date ideas to cover a wide range of hobbies, activities, and interests.

For Homebodies
1. Cook a meal together.
2. Play a board game and rediscover your childhood.
3. Watch a full season of The Andy Griffeth Show on DVD for a TV marathon.

For True Romantics
1. Create love coupons for foot rubs and back massages and cash them in.
2. Go all out with a traditional candlelight dinner.
3. Reserve a B&B getaway.

For Adventure Seekers
1. Spelunking (not the best idea for those afraid of heights).
2. Whitewater rafting.
3. Racecar driving school.

For Artistic Types
1. Take a pottery class.
2. Paint ceramics together.
3. Attend an art show.

For Those Who Love to Learn
1. Take a cooking class and expand your cooking repertoire as a couple.
2. Audit a class on your favorite subject from history to art to marketing.
3. Attend a poetry or book reading.

For Charity Givers
1. Help with bingo night at the local senior citizens' home.
2. Volunteer at the hospital.
3. Take an underprivileged kid to a ballgame or the circus.

For Sports Lovers
1. Watch a minor league game.
2. Join a pickup game in the park, from softball to volleyball to ultimate Frisbee.
3. Take scuba diving or golf lessons.

For Travel Buffs
1. Go for a weekend getaway.
2. Plan a vacation together.
3. Get in the car and drive.

For Family Lovers
1. Double date with the folks.
2. Play charades.
3. Plan and cook a big family dinner.

Works Cited:
Cohen, Jeff (2000) *Dating, Inc.* (World Wide Web
http://p21.pers.re4.yahoo.com/us/static/dating-advice_unique-date)

Harley, Willard F., Jr. (1997) His Needs, Her Needs (Grand Rapids, MI, Baker Book House)

Webb, Michael, (2000) The RoMANtics Guide, (New York, Hyperion)

CHAPTER FOUR

Me?...Quiet?

I recently sat at the dinner table with a group of college students. It seems that one of the female students had, in the midst of a bad day, unleashed her tongue on some well-meaning businessman. She told us of the anger in her voice and the "let him have it" spirit in her words. Then several of the students at the table applauded her saying things like "You go girl!" and "Way to stick up for yourself!"

We live in a world of feminism; a culture which gives its respect to the loudest and most crass of women; a society that gives its nod to the Brittneys and Madonnas who trample the time honored values of modesty, decorum and femininity.

So how do Christian women respond to this world of feminism? Does living in the "I am woman --hear me roar" era give us a pass to ignore scriptures such as the following?

Let no one seek his own, but each one the other's *well-being* (I Corinthians 10:24).

Therefore, whatever you want men to do to you, do also to them, for this is the Law and the Prophets (Matthew 7:12).

Be of the same mind toward one another. Do not set your mind on high things, but associate with the humble. Do not be wise in your own opinion. Repay no one evil for evil. Have regard for good things in the sight of all men. If it is possible, as much as depends on you, live peaceably with all men. Beloved, do not avenge yourselves, but *rather* give place to wrath; for it is written, "Vengeance is mine, I will repay," says the Lord. Therefore "If your enemy is hungry, feed him; if he is thirsty, give him a drink; for in so doing you will heap coals of fire on his head." Do not be overcome by evil, but overcome evil with good (Romans 12:16-21).

When thinking about the latter part of Romans twelve, it serves us well to think about the first two verses of that same chapter. They tell us in no uncertain terms that Christians are to live sacrificial and holy lives. They call us to moral and spiritual nonconformity. They give us a clarion call to be distinctive from the society in which we live. While sometimes when we think of worldliness we think of drinking, illicit sex or reckless affluence, we must remember that worldliness is simply caving in to societal norms. For us, as women in the dawn of the twenty-first century in America, there is no greater temptation to be like the world than that of adapting society's feminist mentality. The devil must surely be gloating over this attitudinal saturation even within the Lord's church. We must guard our hearts, words and decisions from this invasion of culture. We must, like Caleb of old, reject the spirit of our contemporaries and be filled with "another spirit" (Numbers 14:24).

What is that spirit?

Wives, likewise, *be* submissive to your own husbands, that even if some do not obey the word, they, without a word, may be won by the conduct of their wives, when they observe your chaste conduct *accompanied* by fear. Do not let your adornment be *merely* outward—arranging the hair, wearing gold, or putting on *fine* apparel— rather *let it be* the hidden person of the heart, with the incorruptible *beauty* of a meek and quiet spirit, which is very precious in the sight of God. (I Peter 3:1-4).

The spirit described above is the essence of a woman's share in making marriage work. Have you ever considered the change in society that would be affected if women en masse committed themselves to this spirit? Let's prayerfully consider the meaning of a meek and quiet spirit and its amazing implications for our marriages.

What is a meek spirit?

The word Peter uses here means just what you would think: gentle and meek. We know what it means to be a gentle person. It's the way good mothers handle their newborn babies…gently.

It's the way we speak to a godly grandfather who has just lost his companion of sixty years. It's the way we instruct our toddlers to hold the kitten. It's the mildness in our voices as we thank the Father for our safety through a tornado or hurricane. We know what gentleness is.

But what about meekness? Do we have a handle on its definition? Meekness is having a cause bigger than oneself. It's the ability to be about my father's business (Luke 2:49) rather than my own; to fall down before Him and say "not my will but thine be done" (Matthew 26:39); to forever melt my will into His. It is having the heart of Jesus when he said "I am meek and lowly in heart and ye shall find rest unto your souls" (Matthew 11:29). He knew full well that giving me the peace and rest of Calvary meant its torment and agony for Him. Meekness is my ability to put myself—my desires, my comfort, my agenda –aside and find fulfillment in the success of the cause for which I am living. It is being a nonconformist in a self promoting culture.

What is a quiet spirit?

The Greek work for quiet means just that: *quiet and tranquil.* Would this spirit transform our lives or what? Many of our homes are panic-stricken. They often serve as little pit stops between emergencies. When we make those stops it seems we are bombarded with messages, phone calls, emails, and general chaos. My husband, Glenn, recently decided that he wanted to name our house. What he really wanted to do was to use some new woodworking tools and craft a sign for our yard, sort of like the colonial houses often displayed. He even had the name picked out in his mind: *Serenity*. He got busy and made a lovely colonial sign that heralded our visitors that they had arrived at *Serenity*.

He was very proud of his work until one Sunday evening when we got home from worship, some anonymous friend, who likely knew us all too well, had crafted her own wooden sign and had hung it deliberately over the word *Serenity*. It read in large print: *Chaos*. While this was just a neighbor's light-hearted prank, it got me thinking. If the state of my home were printed at all times on a sign in my yard, what would that characterization most often be?

Me?!...Be Quiet?

Tranquility doesn't come to dwell in my spirit accidentally. It takes a conscious decision and deliberate effort. It takes a mind renewal (Romans 12:2) that is truly transforming in nature. Husbands and wives must sit down together and make schedule changes—most often schedule eliminations—that will be conducive to the development of this spirit in the wife. We must ask ourselves what superfluous activities can be eliminated from our schedules. Are there stressful time-consuming projects or practices that would be just as well eliminated? Are there hobbies that need to be put on hold until the children are bigger or even until they are grown? Is there even a second career or job that's not absolutely necessary?

> *Meekness is my ability to put myself – my desires, my comfort, my agenda -aside and find fulfillment in the success of the cause for which I am living. It is being a nonconformist in a self promoting culture.*

And then wives must just commit to this mind renewal. Begin by making sure you have a few minutes of tranquil time in the Word of God each day. Pray daily. Pray fervently. Pray short prayers in the midst of those chaotic times and pray long prayers in those times of quiet reflection. Pray specifically for those issues that bring stress to your life. I Peter five, verse seven tells us to "cast [our] cares on Him, for He cares for [us]." That literally means He will do the caring *for* us or *instead of us*. Pray for wisdom in eliminating unnecessary schedule eaters. Pray for unity in your marriage as you work toward tranquility in your home. Pray that material concerns will always take a back seat to spiritual priorities. Pray every morning. Pray every night. Pray all day.

Practically speaking...

Although every woman must stop and take a good hard look at her life, determining what measures can be taken to make life more peaceful and to calm her spirit, there are a few spirit softeners to which I can attest in my personal life. These are certainly not Biblical injunctions, but they are a few things which have nudged us away from chaos and nearer serenity.

1. Soft background music playing in the house through our days.

2. Fragrant candles burning when the husband/kids come home.

3. The family all present around a dinner table without the TV on.

4. Bickering banished. Children are separated and punished consistently for this infraction.

5. Time invested in home keeping (organization, cleanliness, warmth, nurturing foods, kind notes in lunches, hot cocoa on cold days, etc.).

6. Regularity in bedtime, getting up time, family Bible time, etc. RITUALS!

7. Traditions at holidays that uniquely belong to your little family unit.

8. Refraining from discussing important issues or making big decisions during PMS.

9. Regular husband duty for children. (Once a week or every two weeks, the husband takes the kids and Mom gets to have just two hours at the park, the mall, antiquing, or with a friend.)

10. An occasional night with the phone off the hook or letting the answering machine take all calls. No computer or TV on these nights.

11. The schoolwork rule:All school assignments must be completed before children are allowed to watch any TV or be on the computer at all.

12. Playing the quiet game. If all else fails, this works for at least a few minutes. It works especially well in the car. The driver is the judge and everybody else must remain as silent as possible for thirty minutes. The winner gets a quiet prize, like a puzzle, a word search book, or even a drink at the next drive through restaurant.

13. The goodbye rule. When someone is leaving the house, everybody else gets a personal, look-in-the-eyes goodbye. This promotes harmony and reduces the possibility that someone may tragically leave this life in the midst of unresolved conflict.

Revolutionary Results

If we really work to develop a meek and quiet spirit that truly pervades our activities and interactions, we will soon realize that the effects of such a spirit are phenomenal. Not only will our family members benefit from a more peaceful and serene atmosphere, but their friends will soon discover that our homes are secure and comfortable places to be. Your children will enjoy having their friends, and though their friends may at first think it strange that you actually sit down for meals together, have a family Bible time, and somehow exist most of the time with the TV off, they will love the security of knowing that no one yells at anyone else, ever, in your house. Your home will be a popular hang-out for people of all ages.

You will discover that evangelism is easier than ever. Remember meekness is having a cause that engulfs all of you. Speaking in gentle tones to people inside and outside of your home about the Lord will become a natural part of surrendering to this cause. Soon you will find yourself looking for opportunities to interject the name of Jesus to friends who respect you for your kindness.

You will become less and less concerned about externals and more and more concerned about your inner beauty. Your spirit will slowly become far more radiant and obvious to those around you as you spend more time in front of the mirror of the soul.

But this is a marriage book. The text, I Peter 3: 3-4, is a text written specifically for wives who are attempting to reach their husbands for the Lord. So how will a meek and quiet spirit help my marriage?

It will enhance communication. If I am constantly in a panic, churning on the inside, or waiting to unleash my rage, it becomes increasingly difficult for my husband to do what is often difficult for husbands in the first place ...talk. Communication is the basis for any healthy marriage relationship. If I have a disposition of meekness, my husband perceives a constant invitation to share his world with me. Then when there are difficulties in the relationship, I have, through frequent and intimate conversations built a bridge of comfort and trust. It will be much easier for him to be totally honest with me about his shortcomings, failures and fears. It will be much more difficult for him to have private pockets of his life that are cancerous to married life.

It will help me to be submissive. The benefits and blessings of submission in marriage are discussed in detail in another chapter. It will suffice for now to say that submission and respect are vital to the success of marriage, but they do not occur accidentally. They occur as a natural outgrowth of a meek and quiet spirit. As is generally the case, the behavior follows the attitude. The root word of disposition is dispose. It is my spirit, my disposition, that disposes me to act. I must change my thinking in order to change my life. As a man thinketh in his heart, so is he (Proverbs 23:7).

Think about it:

1. Have class members name women of scripture that they consider to be gentle. Why is each woman cited? Are there certain actions that result from having a gentle spirit? Is the spirit of gentleness identified most by words or actions?

2. How has modern society made it difficult for us to have extended periods of rest and renewal at home? Are there measures we can take to counteract this invasion of society? List at least two activities that steal your serenity that could be eliminated.

3. Are there class members who have additional suggestions for making home a more tranquil haven? List and distribute these ideas.

4. Given the definition of meek, name some Biblical and historical figures who were meek people.

5. How does meekness pave the way for marital submission? Is it a husband's responsibility to be meek as well? Prove your answer Biblically. Can a husband be a good leader without a spirit of meekness? Will a wife be the leader in the home if she is meek? Does meekness affect financial decisions in the home?

Take Me Away

Take me away from the whining,
The fussing of toddlers in tow,
The teasing and tattling, the fussing and prattling
That follows wherever I go.

Take me away from the deadlines;
This appointment, this memo, this bill.
Take me away from the calendar clutter.
Help me, O Lord, to be still.

Take me away from the phone, Lord;
It steals moments that turn into days.
Take me away from these thieves of my time.
Show me a quiet place of praise.

Take me away from this laundry;
That pile on the couch that needs folding;
That bottomless hamper of dirty ones, Lord,
And the load from the dryer I'm holding.

Take me away from the needy,
For often my needs I neglect.
Give me a release—just a small space of peace;
One moment to calmly reflect.

Take me away to your word, Lord;
To the wonderful solace of prayer.
Then hasten me back to the clutter and noise,
For then I can hear Your voice there.

It's then I can see in the eyes of a child
The heritage you've given me.
And here on a crowded calendar page,
There are chances, if only I'll see.

Chances to give some of You, Lord
To someone who's wandering still;
Chances to teach and chances to reach
Into hearts that don't yet know Your will.

Chances to listen, chances to walk
Through doors You have opened for me;
To find souls that are bleeding...souls desperately needing
The Christ of the Mount Calvary.
So take me away, Lord. Renew me.
But don't let me be gone very long.
If I stand very still while in tune to Your will,
I can hear in the clamor, a song!

Cindy Colley

In This Century?!

I recently read about a French teacher who was discussing with her students the use of gender in the French language. She explained that, in French, all nouns are either masculine or feminine. *House*, for instance, is feminine: *la maison*. *Pencil* is masculine: *le crayon*. The students asked about the noun *computer*. The teacher was unsure about the gender of the word, so she divided the students into two groups; one male group and one female group. She asked them to creatively decide which gender they thought the word should be and to give reasons for their conclusions. The results were as follows:

The male group decided that computers should be feminine because:

1. No one but their creator can understand their internal logic.

2. The native language they use to communicate with other computers is incomprehensible to almost everyone else.

3. Even the smallest mistakes are stored in long term memory for possible later retrieval.

4. As soon as you make a commitment to one, you find yourself spending half your paycheck on accessories for it.

The female group was sure computers should be masculine in gender:

1. They have a lot of data, but they are still clueless.

2. They are supposed to help you solve your problems, but half the time they ARE the problem.

3. As soon as you commit to one, you realize that if you'd waited a little longer, you could have gotten a better model.

Of course, the above anecdote is related tongue-in-cheek. Its point is all too obvious. WE ARE DIFFERENT! The one thing that God saw that was not good at the end of His creation of this universe was a man –alone. Woman was created to fill a void. She was the missing piece of the universe puzzle and the blank space where the puzzle piece neatly fit was beside man. She was shaped, physically, emotionally, psychologically and spiritually to "match" the empty puzzle space and fit neatly in the void space beside the man. The very purpose of woman's creation demanded that she be different from man.

But you aren't reading this chapter to learn that we are different. You don't have to major in human anatomy to know that we are physically different. God's purpose in designing our bodies for sexual fulfillment and varying parenting roles is obvious and wonderful. But the difference is far more than a physical one. We think differently. For the past twenty years you've been hearing how women are from Venus and men are from Mars. Although the difference in the sexes is not a planetary difference, it was an intentional difference planned, ordered and perfected by the planet maker. Scientific research in recent years has confirmed that because of neurological differences, men are more logical while women are more emotional in their thinking processes. But married people didn't need scientific research to point this out. While we paint with a broad brush, we understand that generally men tend to examine evidence and make decisions based on the facts: A is true. B is true. Thus we should follow course C.

Their wives can understand the logic. They know that A and B are true. They understand that choice C only follows. But choice C doesn't *feel* right. It is likely to hurt someone's *feelings* and "I just don't *feel* good about C." Emotion trumps logic in a woman's psyche.

His ways are higher than our ways (Isaiah 55:9). His book, although very emotional, is logic based. It is about an understandable and flawless plan, the scheme of redemption, to answer man's desperate need for salvation from sin. Husbands, as spiritual leaders should be drawn to the logic of God's plan of salvation, while wives are the gentle leaders of the fragile souls of children in that vast plan. I don't have to understand why God made us to ink differently. I don't have to understand why He assigned us different roles in the home. But it is fascinating when I see the connection.

Another difference is the ability of men to see the big picture...to focus on long-term goals...while women are masters of detail. That is why when Glenn and Cindy Colley write a book together about marriage, Glenn maps out the chapter titles, and, in his writing, gets straight to the logical point from scripture. Cindy, on the other hand, (the slow-moving hour hand) takes forever, poring over illustrations and poems and details of wording. The differences in our academic make-up produces many varied practical differences in our day to day living...differences that make us complete and whole as one (Genesis 2:24) in the marriage union.

Perhaps one of the most formidable practical challenges in marriage comes from our tasking differences. Men are focused creatures. They tend to think only about one thing at the time, while women are capable of multi-tasking. I've read this in books, but I didn't need a psychologist to inform me of this glaring difference. Women, generally, should learn to save their breath during the football game, for instance. When it's Saturday night and Glenn is working on the Sunday sermon, it's not a good time to ask which shoes are better with the blue dress. Focus is the key word when it comes to accomplishing tasks in a man's world.

Women are multi-taskers. I can cook supper, while working on a math problem with a middle-schooler at the kitchen counter, while feeding the dog, answering the door, reading a recipe to a friend on the phone, and addressing an envelope. I often talk to two people on two different phone lines while I talk to two or three people in the room with me and collect a package from the UPS man at the door. It's just the way God made us. Since we are the "detailers" in the home, this ability to multi-task is a great blessing! Of course, we must challenge ourselves to focus when it's important to focus. We *can* plan tomorrow's menu, rehearse a conversation we plan to have with the PTA president, plan the wardrobe for the trip next week, and make a mental grocery list while being sexual with our husbands. But we shouldn't. We *can* take note of Susan's new haircut, wonder why Sister Slayden is wearing that short-sleeved dress in the dead of winter, think about whether or not we brought the coupons for the restaurant, and decide who the new elders should be—all while we sing "Take time to be Holy", but we shouldn't!

The differences are not subtle. They are fundamental and manifest themselves in obvious and practical ways. The differences are huge obstacles to the modern feminist. But to the Christian couple, seeking fulfillment in God's grand scheme, the differences are dramatic displays of God's wisdom. He made us. He gifted our bodies and minds with the optimum capacities to operate in the roles He assigned. If we determine to do marriage His way, the Great Designer merges our different natures to provide a oneness that elevates our marriages to be the most fulfilling of all human relationships. We can live in the very foyer of heaven itself!

My Role of Submission...

We can lie, beg, cry and flirt our way into almost anything we want... But we can also choose not to be manipulative wives

I'd rather write about hospitality, the fruits of the Spirit, child-rearing or time management...anything but submission. Our culture has beaten down the Christian perspective of marital submission relentlessly in the last four decades. Feminism has intimidated us to even speak of our Biblically submissive roles. Satan has blockaded our days with arenas of embarrassment...places where it seems terribly antiquated and even funny to say, "I am submissive to my husband," or "I obey my husband." The women with whom I work out at the gym would never let me live it down if I said something like that. Tele-marketers have even scoffed at me because I told them I needed to ask my husband before I make a large monetary commitment. How long has it been since you saw a female celebrity profess that she lives under the authority of any man? Oprah doesn't applaud the obedient woman as the model for society.

When I write and speak about submission I pray for boldness to say the Will of God, because, frankly, the Will of God about submission has been dismissed by our culture. I can often see in the eyes of my audiences that I am saying something they have not been hearing in their classes and from their pulpits. But I will continue to teach Biblical submission for two reasons. First, the Bible teaches it. Second, we are not doing it.

Here they are…the only reasons we need as Christians.

1. Ephesians 5:22: "Wives submit to your own husbands as to the Lord…"

2. Ephesians 5:24: "Therefore, just as the church is subject to Christ, so let the wives be to their own husbands in everything."

3. Ephesians 5:33: "…let the wife see that she respects her husband."

4. Colossians 3:18: "Wives, submit to your own husbands as is fit in the Lord."

5. I Peter 3:1: "Wives, likewise, be submissive to your own husbands, that even if some do not obey the word, they, without a word, may be won by the conduct of their wives."

6. I Peter 3:5: "For in this manner, in former times, the holy women who trusted in God also adorned themselves, being submissive to their own husbands."

7. I Peter 3:6: "…as Sarah obeyed Abraham, calling him lord, whose daughters you are if you do good and are not afraid with any terror…"

8. Titus 2:3-5: "The older women likewise…that they admonish the young women to be…obedient to their own husbands, that the word of God may not be blasphemed."

Did you notice the straightforward nature of these injunctions? Did you feel the strength of words like *obey, submit, submissive* and *respect*? See, you and I can argue that submission in our culture is extremely difficult. We can argue that it doesn't really fit into our evolving society. But we cannot argue that it's not commanded in the New Testament.

Oh, there are those who argue that Paul's and Peter's instructions about submission were limited in scope; that these injunctions were intended to apply only to the particular culture to which they were addressed rather than to broadly apply to all cultures thereafter. But this argument has no scriptural merit. Examine closely the instructions of I Timothy 2:11-14. Though these verses more specifically apply to submission to male authority in worship, the principle of origin is applicable to our study.

> Let the woman learn in silence with all subjection.
> But I suffer not a woman to teach, nor to usurp authority over the man, but to be in silence.
> For Adam was first formed, then Eve.
> And Adam was not deceived, but the women being deceived was in the transgression.

Whatever the reason for this submission, it originated in the Garden of Eden. Its application began with Adam and Eve. The principle was in effect during the lifetime of Sarah (I Peter 3: 6) and continued to the culture of the apostles. Since we are instructed to be subject to our husbands as "the church is subject to Christ" (Ephesians 5:24), surely the principle is still binding. Different people...different eras of time…vastly different cultures and societal norms. One universal teaching of the God of all cultures. The origin of this submission teaching is not culture. The origin is creation!

So How Do I Do It?

Obviously the first step is attitude. I have to want to be molded into the submissive wife. This step is huge, but for the purposes of practicality (and because we studied this spirit in the previous lesson), let's assume that we all possess the yielding, moldable heart that God requires to make us His women in the home. Where do we begin? What do we DO to be submissive in a culture that pressures, prods and provokes female leadership in the home? Let's attempt to put a face on the concept of respect with some do's and don'ts that we, with lots of effort and patience, can practice at home.

Dos for respect:

1. Do use respectful terms in conversation with him.

I Peter 3:5 makes it clear that it was important how Sarah spoke to Abraham and even what she called him in their conversations. The passage goes on to say that we can be her spiritual daughters if we put on these conversational characteristics in our marriages. While the appropriate respectful term for my husband in this culture is not "lord", I can easily think of some ways to respect him when we talk. I recall early in our marriage, my southern way to criticize his oversights or mistakes was to say, "Oh Glenn, you beat all!" While this was, in my book, a mild and somewhat playful way to show my disapproval, I remember one day Glenn said, "Cindy, would you please try not to say 'you beat all' to me anymore. It sounds condescending to me." I don't say this anymore. We all can figure out that words like *idiot, numbskull, dummy, fool* and *brainless* are not the modern equivalent of *lord.* Maybe the modern equivalent of calling Glenn my lord would be acknowledging to him that he is my *hero*, my *leader*, my *head* in our home. I try not to say "duh" or "hello?!" when Glenn makes a point that was already obvious to everyone in the room. Some of these phrases may be said in a playful way without being terms of condescension in your home. But we can use our heads and figure out when we are crossing the line of disrespect and learn to rephrase before we violate principles of submission. That's part of learning to live together in knowledge (I Peter 3:7,8).

2. Do be discreet and complimentary when speaking about him to others.

My dear friend Penny is wonderful. But to hear her tell it, she owes every bit of goodness, culture, and grace in her life to her husband, Bill. I recall one night when we were over at Bill and Penny's house for supper, the conversation led by Penny, just kept coming back to the same subject: handsome, caring, wonderful Bill.

When we got into the car to come home, I turned to Glenn and said, "Don't you just get a little tired of hearing Penny gush about

Bill?", to which he responded, "I like it when wives go on about their wonderful husbands." This was a bit of husbandly advice that has served me well. Just as respect for God involves my reflecting that honor for him to others, respect for my husband involves my speaking about him in positive terms.

Don't be tempted to join the wife crowd when they get into the "husband bashing" conversations that seem to be a part of our culture. I'm amazed when I speak at ladies retreats how often conversations during late night game time can digress into times when we laugh at the incompetence of our husbands. Sometimes these stories even involve intimacies that should be kept between husband and wife. When you are tempted to open up the secret places of your marriage, remember the golden rule. Would you want your husband to share what goes on in your bedroom with the guys? We don't have to think about that one!

3. Do everything he asks of you.

I have spoken with those who believe the submission principle only applies to spiritual concerns within the home. When I first discussed this with a friend I must admit that I was intrigued by the idea that the budget might not fall under the submission clause. Upon studying the scriptures, though, I was convicted that submission is not a clause; it's the whole contract.

Think with me for a moment about I Peter 3:1, 2. It says "Wives, likewise, *be* submissive to your own husbands, that even if some do not obey the word, they, without a word, may be won by the conduct of their wives, when they observe your chaste conduct *accompanied* by fear." Here the command to be subject to my husband is given in the context of possibly bringing the unbelieving husband to Christ. The clear injunction to the despondent wife of an unbeliever is to be subject to Him. In what areas does a Christian wife submit to a heathen husband? Well, it wouldn't be in spiritual concerns! In fact, the only *exception* to the submission principle would be a case in which I was asked by my husband to violate God's will in my life. The absurdity of the belief that submission applies only in spiritual matters is highlighted in these verses. But it is clear in other passages as well. Notice the all inclusive language of Ephesians 5:24: "Therefore, just as the church is subject to Christ, so let the wives be to their own husbands **in everything.**"

As I travel and speak to teen girls, I emphasize that there are no loopholes in God's submission contract. There is no small print. That's why it's imperative to marry someone who loves the Lord with all of His being. It is a lifelong blessing to bask in submission to a godly leader who loves you as Christ loved the church (Eph. 5:25). But it's not a good life when you wake up one morning and realize you've placed yourself in submission to one who is selfish and sinful. Lots of time, deliberation and careful observance should be given before we enter the submission contract. (But that's another book.)

Let me reiterate that the one and only time a wife is permitted to disobey her husband is in the case of his insistence that she disobey God. Sapphira should have blown the whistle on Ananias in Acts 5. Sarah should have bucked Abraham's plan of deceit in Genesis 12. Apostolic Inspiration says "we ought to obey God rather than men," (Acts 5:29). I Corinthians 7: 13-14 instructs a woman with an unbelieving husband who refuses to tolerate her Christianity, to let him walk away from her rather than to forsake her Lord. God is my supreme and primary authority. All authority He has delegated must be secondary.

Let me also hasten to add that my husband does not tell me what kind of cookies to bake for the children. He does not make out the grocery list or buy the clothes. He does not even like to make decisions about window treatments or furniture placement, and he abhors choosing a restaurant. He *dwells with me according to knowledge* (I Peter 3: 7), giving me honor. I truly believe he strives to love me as Christ loved the church. When a husband loves his wife in this way, the delegated responsibilities with which she is entrusted are joyful ones. The exemption from bearing the primary responsibility for the family's leadership is liberating. The balance is nothing short of divine perfection.

4. Do be loyal to commitments made to your husband.

Proverbs 31:21 says of the virtuous woman, "The heart of her husband doth safely trust in her." When you've promised to eat lunch with your husband, keep the promise. Don't decide at the last minute you'd rather call up a girlfriend and go to the mall. Only in rare cases in which you know your husband would want you to make another choice would you preempt a time you've promised to him-- The baby woke up sick; Your mom from Quebec is passing through town; The plumber is coming at last to fix the bathroom leak. Even in these cases, don't stand him up. Make sure you both agree on the cancellation of your date. If you've agreed to be in bed together at 10:00 pm tonight, then break your neck to get there. Bottom line: Make sure your husband knows that in his world of broken promises and failures to deliver, there is one person he can count on.

5. Do stay in the budget.

Wholeness, completeness, and competency for a man lies largely in adequate provision for his family. Is this the way it ought to be? Is a healthy man who doesn't provide for his family really a failure? Well, somebody who is *worse than an infidel* (I Timothy 5:8) would not be considered successful. But I, as his wife, can contribute to the wholeness and add to the feeling of competency in my husband by being prudent and frugal. Conversely, I can rob my husband of this wholeness by constantly overspending and keeping financial stability beyond his reach. "A prudent wife is from the Lord" (Proverbs 19:14).

Many times in counseling situations, I've heard wives make statements similar to the following:

> *We've been married for nine years and we're still living in the same little two bedroom house on High Street. It seems like everyone else who was originally in Jerry's department at work has long since been promoted, but not Jerry. We started out in exactly the same financial shape as Lisa and Rick, but look at them now. They've been able to move to a better neighborhood, their kids are in better schools and when I go shopping with Lisa, she can buy without worrying about how much money is in the bank. I just wish Jerry could get us to that point.*

Ladies, never, ever, ever let your Jerry hear you make such a comparison. Jerry needs to be creatively pursuing the best financial status possible for your family (another chapter). But your job is to encourage Jerry, appreciate Jerry, and creatively plan to stay within the family budget made possible by Jerry's salary. I know from my early days of marriage, when both of us were in school and trying to make ends meet on a meager youth minister's weekly check, that this may be very challenging at times. These lean times are when a woman's creativity and ingenuity can shine brightest. I remember my Christmas gifts to family and friends during this time were all handmade items wrapped in Corn Flakes boxes. But they were treasured by the recipients. I was blessed to have a frugal mom who taught me that wonderful treasures can be found for a small fraction of the cost at yard sales, consignment stores and thrift marts (still my favorite!). I learned to clip coupons. Sometimes we just had to say no when our friends were going out to eat. Our home was open to many people, but sometimes we had a big pot of pinto beans and a big pan of cornbread and an onion to serve our guests. The large group of young people we worked with in this congregation spent many hours in our little house. But they knew they all had to bring wieners and chips to our cook-outs. These were some of the most fun days of our marriage. They left a permanent mark deep inside of me. I still find it very difficult to make a clothing purchase until it's at least 75% off. I feel victorious if I wait until it's 80% off of the markdown price at Dillard's and I also have that extra 20% off coupon from the paper. Then when I show my husband my bargains I try to remember to say, "Thank you for making it possible for me to buy nice things for our family." He usually responds by saying, "No. Thank you for being so diligent to find the most incredible bargains."

Of course, it goes without saying that, as Christians, our first financial priority is our giving to the church purposefully and generously each Lord's day. I can promise you that your budget will not be working properly if this is not the case in your house.

6. Do listen when he is talking.

This one seems like a "gimme", but in reality, just listening is one of our biggest challenges. It's because of that multi-tasking talent that we women have. He starts telling me about a business decision that his team is going to make tomorrow at work. I listen for the first paragraph, but subconsciously realize that this is not as interesting as the sale at the mall, so while he talks, I make a mental list of the stores I'm going to try to hit tomorrow, which leads me to think about the fact that the gas tank in the car is empty, which leads me to think about why ARE gas prices so high

(?) and whether or not I should be going all the way to the other side of town tomorrow just for fun shopping…

Suddenly he stops talking. I know his last line was, "So which option d'ya think should get my vote?" I have no clue what the options are (except the option to go to the mall or not)!

I say something like, "Well, what are *you* thinking?"

He says, "I can see good things about both choices."

I say, "Yeah, that's kinda' what I was thinking."

Now I've not only failed to respect him enough to listen. I've lied.

Then he says, "Well, I guess we'll just have to go ahead and sign the contract after we add that clause."

I say, "I guess so."

He says, "How long should we give them in the clause to change the policy?"

You are back at square one. Listening in the first place instead of playing detective now would have been a lot easier *and* a lot more respectful. Always remember, there may be a pop quiz at the end of his dissertation. Most importantly, always remember to honor him. If I got the chance to meet the president of the United States and he asked my opinion about a decision, I think I would honor him enough to respectfully listen. God has directed my honor to this man I chose as my head. "Let every [woman *cc*] be swift to hear, slow to speak…(James1:19).

Don'ts for respect:

1. Don't do whatever it is that gets under his skin.

It might not be the exact same action for you as it is for me. But we all know what annoys our husbands. It is annoying to my husband when I set my alarm for 6:00 a.m. and then hit the snooze till 7:00 a.m. when he doesn't have to get up till 7:00. It annoys him when I leave the house for a couple of hours and leave all the lights on. It annoys him when I remind him to eat his greens in front of the children. (He, like the children, doesn't like greens.) After a short time being married, most women could easily make a list like I've just made. We can choose to refrain from being annoying and, with a little practice, we will become lots more attractive to our husbands.

The writer of Proverbs says there are four things that *the earth* cannot bear. It says these things perturb the earth. One of these four things is a hateful woman when she is married (Pro. 30:21-23). The King James translates hateful *"odious,"* which means obnoxious. Sometimes I need to look at my little annoying habits and ask myself, "Am I odious?"

2. Don't give him the silent treatment.

The way God ordered the home and designed our psyches makes women the emotional tone-setters. This fact has far-reaching implications.

Do you ever have evenings at home when you don't speak to one another? Someone's miffed because of some slight or some frustrated statement. A few misunderstood statements have been exchanged. Maybe there was no explosion or anger, but still, there's something in the air between you. You are distant and cool. At least one of you is pouting.

Our very good friends, Bud and Lucille, were happily married for about thirty-five years. Little did Bud know that night, when he kneeled beside the bed and prayed with Lucille, that she would not awaken in the morning. Following the prayer, he leaned over and kissed her, they exchanged "I love you's" and went to sleep. It was just a regular night. It was only the next morning, when Bud brought Lucille her coffee in bed that he discovered her spirit had left. He just slowly sat down beside her and said, "Oh Lucille, you've gone on and left me."

All of our nights should be like this…just regular nights. One day someone will leave someone and we don't know which regular night it might be. But surely all of us would want it to be a night like this. There is wisdom in the words of Ephesians 4:26: Let not the sun go down on your wrath. I would add: Don't let the car leave the garage on your wrath. Don't put the phone receiver down on your wrath. Don't close an email on your wrath. Glenn and I recently met our close friend, Cindy, at the hospital moments after her husband had been in a wreck on his way home from work, only to agonize with her as the hospital personnel brought the wedding ring from his finger and gave it to her. From there we went to tell her children that their father had died. Cindy bravely faced the realities and was amazingly strong as we told the children. As tough as things were that day for her, they were not nearly as unbearable as they could have been had there been problems in their relationship as he left the house that morning. But our God shields us, as His children, from the biggest pains of life and death. When we are doing life and marriage His way, the biggest of burdens are blessed with peace and hope. Not only do we live prepared for the worst eventuality, but the everyday living is blessed with peace and serenity as well. It takes effort, but daily pout resistance pays big dividends.

3. Don't feel the need to censor his conversation for correctness.

Those of us who are parents know all too well how annoying and sometimes even humiliating it is to have a child constantly interrupting our conversation with another adult to correct the details of our conversation:

"No, mom, it wasn't last Wednesday. We went there on Tuesday."

"No mom, that wasn't at Jenny's game. That happened at my game."

"We weren't having a hamburger cookout. Remember? Dad grilled hot dogs."

To say the least, conversation flows much more smoothly without the interruptions. That's one of the characteristics of adult conversation for which we moms long throughout our days. It's not hampered by questions, detours, and interruptions.

You and I have seen wives who can hardly let their husbands utter a sentence without interjecting some correction or missed detail. Not only are they conversation dominators, but they have a way of making their husbands appear very foolish in the process.

This is not respectful. It is childish and demeaning. Not only will it frustrate his exchanges with others, but it will slowly erode the communication process between the two of you. I've been around some husbands who've become withdrawn and private whenever they are around their wives. The risk of stating an opinion or relating a story is just not worth the bother.

At this point, interjection has escalated to contention. It may seem as if your constant clarifications are just helping him get it right. But those corrections can effectively shut down the communication flow that's vital to marital happiness.

"Better to dwell in the wilderness, than with a contentious and angry woman" (Pro. 21:19).

"A continual dripping on a very rainy day and a contentious woman are alike; Whoever restrains her restrains the wind, and grasps oil with his right hand" (Pro.27:15-16).

Of course, if you hear your husband inadvertently mislead or even lie to someone, you must address this with him. But this confrontation should be done first in private if at all possible.

4. Don't manipulate.

All women possess the tools for manipulation. Delilah (Judges 16) was a genius of it. We can lie, beg, cry and flirt our way into almost anything we want. We can withhold sexual pleasure or feign sexual pleasure to achieve our small purposes. But we can also choose not to be manipulative wives. There is nothing about manipulation that fits into *respect, submit,* or *obey*.

5. Don't take big matters into your own hands.

It's always better to hear, "Sure, that's fine with me," than "I can't believe you didn't ask me before you did that." Some of you are thinking, "This sounds like it's from another century." It is. It was the Holy Spirit in the first century, who said that wives must be subject "to their husbands in every thing" (Ephesians

5:24). Remember when it all started...back in the garden (I Timothy 2:11-14)? Remember how it was for Sarah's time, too (I Peter 3:5,6)? It's a part of God's transcendent plan for all people of all time. He made us and He still knows best. We can still do it His way and be blessed. The alternative, living outside His Will, is one of those *ways that seems right to a woman* (Prov.16:25) in my century, but I don't like what's at the end of that way.

In the final analysis...

As we remember who it was that laid down this submission law in the first place, let's also remember that it's the same Holy Spirit who will be blasphemed if we choose to ignore it (Titus 2:3-5). I believe we are witnessing a large scale blasphemy regarding this principle in our society today. We can choose to offer our lifestyle's assent to this blasphemy or to be reverently directing our lives to honor His Holy Word.

Think About It:

1. Have a class member research the Greek words for honor, obey, reverence and submit from the passages listed in this lesson. Have him bring the definitions of these words to class to share.

2. Would it be more difficult for a Christian woman who is married to a non-Christian husband to live faithfully than it would be for a Christian man who is married to a non-Christian wife? Discuss the reasons for your conclusion.

3. Why is it so hard for women to listen? Give examples of how a failure to listen can be damaging in the marriage relationship. Then cite Bible passages that teach good listening skills.

4. Make a personal (and private) written list of the things that annoy your husband. Make a conscious effort in the next week to avoid these things.

5. From Titus 2, we find that it is our responsibility both to do and to teach the submission principle to prevent blasphemy of the Holy Spirit. Do you think it's more difficult to do or to teach? Why?

When It's Hard

If I submit when it's easy…
When it makes sense to me,
Doing God's Will when I think it best,
I don't really obey.
I'm just having my way.
When it's difficult…there lies the test.

When the culture screams one thing,
The Word whispers another,
When I can't understand that command;
When I wriggle and wrest
But I know His way's best,
That's the time when I'm under His hand.

Faith is not faith when
You see why it works.
When you know why each move you are making.
The steps that are guiding
To where He's providing
Are the ones I don't know why I'm taking.

He's saved all His best
For His children of faith,
But the best is not yet for beholding.
When my eyes are too weak
For the heaven I seek
I just trust in the Hand I am holding.

Cindy Colley

CHAPTER SIX

Committed Love

"Of course I love my wife."

Just what do you mean when you say that? After hearing a sermon on what the Bible actually says about wives' submission to their husbands, men may feel that they have a role that requires less adjustment and that they should pretty much do what comes naturally. But before you fall for that misconception, let's look at the real definition of husbandly love. Brace yourself. Love, done the Biblical way, is a formidable challenge for the average husband.

Start with Ephesians 5:25. It gives the explicit command: "Husbands. love your wives…" There are four main Greek words for love, each with a distinctive meaning. phileo, storge, eros, and agape. The command is for husbands to *agape* their wives. The King James uses the word *charity*, and perhaps that's a good translation, for agape is love based not on the value of the recipient, but on the character of the giver. It is sometimes called "Christian love" because it is the love which makes us want to do what is best for everyone around us—even our enemies (Matt. 25:44).

The Holy Spirit really wanted us to have a grasp on this little word, "agape," so He gave us a whole chapter on it. I Corinthians 13 is on a completely different subject than marriage, but whether you are speaking of brothers enjoying unity in the church, or husbands enjoying unity with their wives, agape is the answer. In this chapter we find a general principle with a specific example. The general principle is what we want to see today. Just what is agape love? Observe the descriptions of love which have a direct bearing on the happiness of our marriages:

Love Suffers Long

Another translation says love is *patient..* This Greek word, as used in the New Testament, always describes patience with people and not patience with circumstances. It is the word used of the man who is wronged and who has it easily in his power to avenge himself and yet will not do it; one who is slow to anger. It is seen when a man works to exercise the same patience as God has already shown us.

Wikipedia, an internet encyclopedia, states that no one treated Abraham Lincoln with more contempt than a man named Edwin Stanton. Stanton observed that no one needed to travel to Africa to capture a gorilla because he could easily find one in Springfield, Illinois. Lincoln said nothing, but later made Stanton his war minister because he was the best for the job. Years passed. The night of Lincoln's death Stanton looked down at Lincoln's still face and with tears remarked, "There lies the most perfect ruler of men the world has ever seen." Lincoln respected Stanton without regarding the fact that Stanton wished him ill.

Sir, are you patient with your wife when she makes mistakes? When she is worn thin? When she has PMS, nothing seems to go right, and she feels she can't seem to accomplish one blessed thing!!? No awards are handed out for patience when she is feeling good and cooperative. The real character shines through when you are patient in tough times. I Peter 3:7 says to dwell with your wife "according to knowledge," and that takes some loving attention to how she is feeling.

Remember agape love rises above circumstances and wants the best for the other person.

Love Is Kind

The early Greek scholar Origen, as quoted by Barklay, said that this means that love is "sweet to all" (pp. 120).

So much Christianity is good but unkind. In John 8:4 the Pharisees brought a woman to Jesus "taken in adultery." They believed they had found the perfect trap for a perfect prophet. "Should we stone her or not?" If He judged her worthy of death, as they believed the law of Moses required Him to do, they could accuse Him before the Romans who reserved the right of capital punishment only for themselves. If He did not require stoning of the woman, they would accuse him before the Jews as a violator of Moses' law.

Jesus was brilliant. He defused the time bomb with "He who is without sin among you, let him throw a stone at her first" (Jn. 8:7). They were using the woman. She was nothing to them except a visual for their argument of entrapment for Jesus. They felt no compassionate kindness toward her at all. On whose side would you have been? So many Christians would have sided with the rulers and not with Christ if they had been present with the woman taken in adultery. The Holy Spirit commands us to be kind (Eph. 4:32).

I find it ironic when I see in some Christians a warm kindness shown to outsiders, but a serious lack of kindness in their marriages, as if the rules of Christian living somehow change when I close the door of my own house behind me. Where does the Bible teach that? It doesn't. Think about the overall way you treat your wife. Are you kind to her? If not, you are not obeying the command to love your wife.

Love Doesn't Envy

Envy is a silent problem in day-in-day-out marriage life. One partner really believes the arrangement of work and responsibility is tilted so that he or she has more burdens to bear than the other.

> *For a man to agape-love his wife means that he is a godly leader in his home, a sanctified man.*

Husband, do you ever begrudge the easy life your wife enjoys? Do you ever want to say, "Hon, you've really got it made!" Much of the time, that sentiment could be cured by spending a couple of weeks living her life. God gave husbands and wives specific roles to fill in marriage. His primary role is spiritual leader and breadwinner (I Tim. 5:8). Hers is to care for the home (Tit. 2:4,5). It is foolish to question God's wisdom in this perfect design. Granted, sometimes mates need adjustments in how they are handling their roles, but if your wife is fulfilling what God asks of her, get envy out of your heart. She would not make a good husband, and you'd make a terrible wife.

Love Does Not Parade Itself, Is Not Puffed Up

To *parade* ones self is to brag, and to be puffed up is to be inflated with one's own importance. I've heard that Napoleon always advocated the sanctity of the home and the obligation of public worship—for others. Of himself he said, "I am not a man like other men. The laws of morality do not apply to me." Talk about puffed up!

There is a self-effacing quality in a Christian husband's agape love. Some husbands give their love with the idea that they are bestowing a favor on their wives. But agape love teaches a man to live grateful that he is so loved. Love is kept humble by the belief that he can never offer her any less than himself to repay her devotion in giving her life in marriage to him. I don't have to wonder if my wife Cindy had other men she could have chosen to marry. I spent considerable effort wooing her from one such suitor to make her mine. She willingly agreed to marry me and that has made all the difference.

Love Does Not Behave Rudely

Another translation of this says that one does not act *grace-lessly*. There are some husbands who take delight in being blunt and almost brutal. Maybe they grew up around a father who treated their mother that way and it's all they've known. Maybe stresses have just built up and courtesy has just been thrown out the window.

There is a graciousness in Christian love which never forgets that courtesy, tact and politeness are lovely things. When did you get the idea that courtesy is something you extend to strangers (do you open the door at a restaurant or store for a woman you don't know?), but not something you typically do for your own wife? Some husbands commonly treat their wives to a mean spirit; a spirit which they would be hesitant to show to anyone else. Does that seem right to you?

Do you ever thoughtlessly embarrass your wife in front of others with your unseemly behavior? Do you sometimes tell jokes in front of others that make fun of her?
Do you remember a time when you took humor too far and hurt her?

Love Seeks Not Its Own

Another translation for this is: "...does not insist upon its rights."

I like what Barclay thought about this. He said,

> "In this world there are but two kinds of people—those who always insist upon their privileges and those who always remember their responsibilities; those who are always thinking of what life owes them and those who never forget what they owe to life. It would be the key to almost all the problems which surround us today if men would think less of their rights and more of their duties" (p. 122).

The final authority for decisions in the home rests with the husband (Eph. 5:23-24). But this doesn't mean the husband always gets his way. He doesn't confront his wife with the Biblical principle of authority to overpower her wishes unless the matter is serious and demands it. For example, he wouldn't reason, "I like this boat; it's a good deal, and I don't have to talk it over with her first. I'm the man of the house after all!" Love seeks not her own. Say hello to selfishness and you'll kiss happiness goodbye!

Love Is Not Easily Provoked

Another translation says, "Love never flies into a temper". Agape love fights the temptation to become easily exasperated with people. No one enjoys being around such a man because you feel a nervous danger in his presence.   Possessing and exhibiting a hair-trigger temper is something you must change to please God and your wife.

Kipling said, "If you can keep your head when all about you are losing theirs and blaming it on you" and "being hated, don't give way to hating...you'll be a man, my son." The man who is master of his temper can be master of anything (Kipling).

How are you doing on tempter-control in your life and especially around your wife?

Love Thinks No Evil

Another translation says, "does not store up the memory of any wrong it has received". This is fascinating.   The Greek word is an accountant's term which amounts to a man entering up an item on a ledger so it won't be forgotten. Are you good at forgetting what you've forgiven or are you more apt to bring history up when you disagree with your wife? One of the great arts in marriage is to learn what to forget. Some people nurse their wrath to keep it warm. They brood over wrongs until it is impossible to forget them. We must work at having a good forgetter.

Paul wrote in Colossians 3:19, "Husbands, love your wives and do not be bitter toward them." Bitterness is stored up grievances, and both husbands and wives would do well to get rid of it. If it's going to happen, bitterness usually surfaces when we are not at our best and become angry with our wives. The matter we're arguing over may start seeming too small to justify the strong feelings inside me. So I start reaching into the sins of my spouse's past to fortify my side of the argument. Fight this temptation. If you and your wife find something on which to disagree, stick to the subject and find a way to work it out. Don't let yourself introduce bitterness and make the matter worse. One husband said to a friend, "Every time my wife and I argue she become historical." The friend said, "You mean hysterical?" He answered, "No, historical. She brings up every wrong thing I've ever done."

Aren't there some things in your past you'd deeply appreciate your wife forgetting and never using against you again? Offer her the same compassion.

Love Does Not Rejoice In Iniquity, But Rejoices In The Truth

Husbands, agape does not enjoy sin in one's self nor in other people. For some, there is a type of pleasure which comes when they hear something sinful about someone else. It makes for good gossip. Would I be more eager to hear something derogatory about someone or something of their good character or fortune?

Is it easier to weep with those who weep or to rejoice with those who rejoice? Aren't there times when the truth is the very last thing we want to hear?

Where this gets practical is in the fact that I am to be spiritual leader of my wife and children. My job is to work to make Cindy an even more radiantly beautiful Christian than she already is, and to see that my home is securely Christian.

Take a look at your family's entertainment choices, what you watch on TV, what you rent at the video store, the web sites you frequent, etc. Are you leading your family in things consistent with a man who doesn't rejoice in iniquity? Gentlemen, it's difficult to say that we don't rejoice in iniquity while we watch the typical R-rated movie or a sitcom which glamorizes homosexuality. In so many homes the wife is the stronger Christian and leads the home in what is right. Sir, that role should be filled by you, a man who loves Jesus and His church and takes manhood seriously.

Do I take an occasional drink? Maybe a cold beer for refreshment when I come in from cutting the lawn or when fishing with friends? If so, I'm failing the test for agape love. Such things will come to no good; not in my marriage, or in my children.

Do I pull my family back from faithful worship attendance? Who is the motivator behind being with the church whenever the church-house doors are open? Is it me or is it my wife?

For a man to agape-love his wife means that he is a godly leader in his home, a sanctified man.

Love Bears All Things, Endures All Things.

Another translation says, "Love can endure anything." In other words, love can bear any insult, any injury, and any disappointment. This describes the kind of love that Jesus had for us. "But God demonstrates His own love toward us, in that while we were still sinners, Christ died for us" (Rom. 5:8).

Sometimes marriage is easy and fun. Other times it is a struggle. What is a man to do when his wife says cutting things? What is he to do when she physically isn't able to do what she once could? What is he to do when she isn't the kind of Christian he hoped she'd be? At those times he must remember the old adage, "It isn't your love that sustains your marriage. It is your marriage which sustains your love." You promised before God that you would be faithful to your wife in good times and bad.

When Jesus taught the Sermon on the Mount He taught us how to avoid retaliation: "You have heard that it was said, 'An eye for an eye and a tooth for a tooth.' But I tell you not to resist an evil person. But whoever slaps you on your right cheek, turn the other to him also" (Mat 5:38-39). How would your marriage improve if neither you nor your wife ever retaliated against the other again? What if, when she has PMS and says something perfectly awful to you, you don't respond in anger? What if, when you come home from work, stressed and ill-tempered, and you say something thoughtless and cruel to her, she doesn't retaliate? How many arguments and harsh words would never be uttered! How hurt feelings could be avoided!

This facet of agape guides us through the hard times.

Love Believes All Things And Hopes All Things

This love is completely trusting. In relation to God it is that love which takes God at His word and takes New Testament promises which say "whosoever" and says, "That means me."

In relation to our fellow man it is our nature to think the best we can about people. Do you think that, to a degree, we make people what we believe them to be? If we show we don't trust them, we may make them untrustworthy. How many great men/women through history were told as children they wouldn't amount to much in one area or another? Love thinks well of people and tries to make some hope out of the threads of possibilities.

Do yourself a favor and apply this to your marriage. Really love your wife by complimenting her good qualities and applauding her achievements. Express confidence in her future. You can do it! A wife whose husband believes in her will be motivated to greater heights.

This component of agape love comes easy for the husband who knows how great it feels to be given the same vote of confidence by his wife.

Think about it:

1. What are the four Greek words for love? How are they different from one another? What is special about Agape?

2. Go back and look at each heading and rank yourself on a scale of one to ten (ten being the highest), first in reference to your acquaintances, then in reference to yourself.

3. What external pressures cause you to be easily provoked or blow up? Talk about these with your wife, and together make a plan for recognizing those and dealing with them.

4. Is there anything in your life right now that is out of sync with the description in
I Corinthians 13, "Love does not rejoice in iniquity"? Asked another way, is there some iniquity in which I'm currently rejoicing?

5. Does the use of pornography violate principles of agape love? Why or why not?

6. Husbands, in your private devotions, type out the description of love in I Corinthians 13 and replace the word love or charity with your own name. Post this where you will read it repeatedly to get this firmly cemented in your heart.

7. Discuss why kindness to strangers, or even friends, is easier than kindness in our families. How can we help this problem in our homes?

The Word I Didn't Mean

There wouldn't be this quietness…
This sadness in my heart;
This distance in her manner…
We're together, but apart.

If I had only thought of this
Before I said that word.
But my tongue is in a slippery place
And once it's out, she's heard.

Oh, I have said, "I'm sorry."
And she said, "It's okay"
She even said she understands
Why I should feel that way.

But tiny words in anger
Escaping in the space between us
Can spawn huge tornadic forces.
That will batter and careen us.

Before they're done, we're aching.
We have wounds to tend and clean
And all because that word escaped…
The one I didn't mean.

Cindy Colley

Works cited:
Barclay, William (1975) Commentary on Corinthians (Philadelphia, PA, Westminster Press)

Kipling [On-line], URL; http://www.bible.org/illus.php.

Wikipedia, [On-line], URL; http://en.wikipedia.org/wiki/Edwin_Stanton.

CHAPTER SEVEN

So What Do You Do All Day?

So here you are. You've turned the page to read the most difficult chapter of the book. The topic at hand is undeniably the most
controversial subject we teach as we conduct marriage and parenting seminars around the country. It is the chapter many people
find objectionable in our parenting book *Your Mama Don't
Dance*. It may seem to you that if this subject causes such a stir,
we should just omit it from our materials and seminars. But there
are several important reasons for broaching this uncomfortable
subject. All of them affect the ultimate success and happiness of
our marriages. So here you are.

What it means:

*The older women likewise, that they be reverent in behav-
ior, not slanderers, not given to much wine, teachers of
good things—that they admonish the young women to love
their husbands, to love their children, to be discreet, chaste,
homemakers, good, obedient to their own husbands, that
the word of God may not be blasphemed" (Titus 2:3-5).*

To be homemakers. It's right there in the same list with discretion, love of husbands and children, chastity, goodness and submission. It precedes the haunting phrase "that the Word of God be
not blasphemed." What does it mean?

Whatever it means, to be a keeper at home is a serious injunction. (Failure to comply results in blasphemy.) Whatever it means,
it's directed to younger women who are married with children.
Whatever it means we are to *do it* when we are young and *teach it*
when we are old.

The Greek word translated *homemakers* is *oikouros*. It's translated *keepers at home* in the King James Version and *workers at
home* in the American Standard Version. Its first definition,

according to Thayer's Greek-English Lexicon of the New Testament is *the watch or keeper of the house.* The verb form of the root word means *keeping at home and taking care of household affairs, domestic* (1977, p.442).

Feminists in our society don't want to see this or be this. But we are not feminists. We are Christians. Our calling is not to the culture, but to the Christ. So whatever the duties and responsibilities implied in the above definition, we take them seriously, believing they are authored by our Creator…the One who knows what is best for our lives…the One whose wisdom transcends time and culture.

So *keepers at home,* just like obedience to husbands or chastity, has got to have a practical application in my life. It means whatever I may be doing in my life, that during the years I have my children at home with me, my career, my first business priority, is taking care of my home and household affairs. I may choose to do this for many reasons, but the number one reason is submission to my God.

How did we come this far?

Day care is a mammoth institution. Its impact on the children who are placed within its care is immeasurable. A child placed in day care at the age of six months who stays until it's time to start school has amassed about eight thousand hours of non-parental caregiver's influence. When we multiply this number of hours by the millions of children who spend their days in center-based care, we are not surprised by the decay of family life in America. For many children, home is just the place for sleeping.

I can read statistics about the massive numbers of children in day care or even about the poor quality of day care centers that, although shocking, seem as if they are describing some urban area far away. "These surveys surely must have been taken in New York City or Los Angeles," I tend to think. "Everybody knows that the children in those huge inner cities are all in government subsidized centers."

And then it happens in my city. It's not a statistic anymore. It's a local newspaper story and it caught my attention one morning at breakfast. At two separate and unrelated day care centers two children left by day care workers in the vans that were to deliver them to the centers in the morning, died on the same day as temperatures climbed into the nineties. I was appalled! I had heard that this happened on one other occasion about two years ago before I moved into the area. But twice in one day in the same city? How many times do children stay in the van all day on cooler days and no one ever even hears about it? If this can happen at two different facilities on the same hot day, how much nurturing—I mean real one-on-one communication and attention—is being given to the kids?

Then a few days later I was reading the same paper and noted that another day care owner in the same town was arrested for DUI while transporting children to his facility. In this instance parents had already reported that he was driving the children while inebriated on another occasion. The owner decided to close the facility and has now applied for a liquor license to open a lounge on his property instead. The following week the story was of a seven-year-old who was left sleeping on the day care van and managed to roll down a window and climb out on her own. Then a front page headline read, "Live baby found in trash bin outside day care—Police believe Mom is employee." Follow-up stories revealed that the mom indeed was an employee. In fact, she was the teacher of a class of three-year-olds. I wonder what values were being transferred in this classroom. I wonder if this teacher would value the safety and well-being of your child more than she did that of her own.

> *In our affluent "No-child-left-behind" world, it seems that many children literally are being left behind by caregivers who are missing one important ingredient: maternal ownership.*

The kicker for me is not that this extreme neglect, abuse, and even murder can happen in large day care centers. It's that the government has to step in to decide whether or not the center stays open. Parents are still game. They're still willing, even as the funeral for their children's little classmate is being planned, to allow their children to return to the same center. The next operating day following the children's suffocation deaths in the day care van, children were still scurrying off to the center in large numbers. Nothing short of a license revocation stops these parents from placing their children in these centers where clearly the proper attention is not being given them! Never in my wildest dreams can I imagine leaving my child in any situation where any degree of neglect has been noted, much less the death of a child due to inattention of day care workers! I don't need a social worker to come in and review this situation and decide for me if this center meets proper standards of safety and accountability. Where are the parents? ...At work, I guess (Colley and Colley pp. 77-78).

Our daughter, Hannah, works at a science museum. Last week she was on duty early one morning to greet a busload of daycare students. Waiting for the bus to arrive, she received a call. "The group from _____ Daycare will be late. We forgot a couple of the kids we were supposed to pick up this morning and we have to go back and get them." When the bus left the museum in the afternoon, once again a child was left behind in the exhibit area. It was a long while before the daycare workers even discovered he was missing. In our affluent "No-child-left-behind" world, it seems that many children literally are being left behind by caregivers who are missing one important ingredient: maternal ownership.

Studies have shown that infants in day care are over twelve times more likely to become infected with meningitis than children kept at home. The incidence of hepatitis has been shown to be directly linked to the environment of the child care facility. The risk of contagion is in direct proportion to the size of the day care facility and the number of hours a child spends there (Dobson and Bauer, 127). These studies alone demand accountability from responsible parents. But they do not even approach the issue of values. What are the contagions of the world with which my children may become infected when they remain in the care of unbelievers?

To be sure, I cannot quote studies and statistics to address the importance of mothers instilling values within the home. But from a practical point of view, I can tell you what I have found to be the case in twenty-seven years of being a preacher's wife. On many occasions Christian parents have come to my husband or to us as a couple in times of family crisis involving teens who are reaping the whirlwind (Hos. 8:7). Often the family is experiencing excruciating pain because of drug involvement, promiscuity or teen pregnancy. Almost always, this deviant behavior that now is obvious to all who love the family began in secret in the afternoon while Mom was at work. While I am not naive enough to believe that the only factor involved in sinful teen behavior is the absence of Mom, thus providing a convenient place for it to occur, I do firmly believe that when we are with our children more, we will know of their temptations, be more fully aware of their behavior, and be more able to intervene before temptation turns to tragedy. (See Proverbs 29:15.) I believe this preventive relationship is developed through years of maternal nurturing (Colley and Colley, 79).

Recently, a sad but common scenario was occurring daily just down the street from me. Each afternoon, a young latch-key girl from the local middle school got off the school bus and let herself in the house. Minutes later, a boy from the high school parked his truck on another street near the house and walked over to the girl's house and entered the back door. Two concerned moms in the neighborhood decided that the girl's mother should at least be informed that her daughter was spending two hours alone in the house with an older boy each afternoon. So we called her at work. She immediately became livid. "Well! That does it!" she said. "Tomorrow that girl goes on birth control!" Well, that response was shocking, to say the least. But it was not as shocking as what next came out of this mother's mouth: "I wish I could just get in the car, come home, and catch her at this business right now. But I can't. I have a hair appointment."

I hope her hair looked really good at the end of that day. I hope her job was extremely fulfilling each day as she worked away at that desk while her daughter's virginity was being forfeited at the tender age of twelve or thirteen. I hope her salary afforded her lots of nice things for her closet and home. I hope she really enjoyed the material affluence and social status of her good job...because this mother paid a very high price for all of those *things*. Things are temporary. Children are eternal.

One teenager recently put it this way: "Mrs. Cindy, my mother said she wished she could stay home and spend her days with me. But she said, if she did, we 'just couldn't have our pool.'" This teenager, unknowingly, hit the nail on the head. At first, our children can quote our materialistic reasons for leaving them alone or in the care of others every day. They can tell us the amenities of affluent living that mom is providing by working. But one day, the truth stares them in their adolescent faces. They come to slowly understand that mom had a choice and her choice was to leave her children in the care of others. Mom *chose* material things over time spent raising me. At some point, they "get it".

More than lip service

We are well into the second generation of children being raised in homes with working moms. In teaching teens the intrinsic value of motherhood, the obstacle that I face is ignorance. Many of the girls have never even heard that it's important for a mother to be at home with her small children. Their moms have always been away and they have no concept of what it would be like to come home from school in the afternoon and communicate with a parent.

Our culture has shouted the significance of career for four decades and we in God's kingdom have been affected. While we still give lip service to the joys of motherhood, we are failing to mentor our girls in practical ways to be godly mothers. While I realize that all of our situations are different, I pray that we will honestly examine our lifestyles and motives to be sure that we are reflecting a commitment to things eternal—not just things.

Our daughters need moms who do more than play games, read stories, and color with them. From early ages we need to involve our daughters in learning homemaking skills. They will learn to love cooking and sewing if given the chance. They will become proficient vacuumers and dusters with a little practice. I know it's easier just to do it yourself than to have to come along behind them and get all the spots they've missed, but before long your patience will pay off. Involve them in hospitality projects and baking for the sick. (Read Proverbs 31 and see how many areas of virtuous womanhood you and your daughter can master together.) In this way the joys of giving that emanate from a godly home will be real to them. At the same time you will be giving them your most valuable commodity—your time. They will always remember this gift (Colley and Colley, 81-82)

Considering options

Sometimes there is not one…a choice, I mean. My friend, Tish, was not a Christian when her daughter Carla was born. In fact she was only a teenager who had been turned out onto the streets at the tender age of twelve. Young, single and alone, she struggles now, after having heard and obeyed the gospel, to make ends meet by working limited hours in a department store to provide the necessities for Carla and still attempt to give her the time that she so desperately needs. Now that Tish knows God's Will for her life, she would love to be able to devote herself fully to the keeper vocation. But, for now, that choice is out of her reach. She does the best she can in the situation in which she finds herself.

Mostly because of the immorality that pervades our society, there are many Tishes among us. But sometimes the problem is a sick or handicapped husband. Sometimes it may be a temporary lay-off or loss of employment. The fact is, sometimes mothers are forced to work, at least for a while, outside the home.

But for most of us in America today, our vocation is a choice. God has placed us in the richest society in the modern world. Many of us have been blessed to attend college and have the credentials to enter the work force in positions that provide enticing salaries. Sometimes the choice to be a keeper at home is a difficult one. But for most of us, when we look at our personal situations, we would have to admit that somewhere along the way, we made a choice to stay at home and raise our children or to seek (or keep) full time employment. When we begin to look at the issue of employment (or not) as a choice instead of an already prescribed way of life, we begin to see options that we never saw before. We see *things* in our lives that we enjoy, but could surely do without. We see expenses in our lifestyles that are actually incurred *because* of our jobs. We see ways that we could supplement the family income from within our homes or by spending a fraction of the forty hour work week outside the home. One friend of mine, a bank executive, began to be haunted by the undone jobs of motherhood and took a much less prestigious job, but one that required a fraction of the time, at her children's school. My sister has taught on the university level, but now chooses to stay home with her four children. She has turned her photography hobby into a small business from her home to supplement the income. My friend, Sherry, thought she had to work until she got a call from the school saying her daughter was ill and needed to be picked up from school. She hurried away from her demanding job and picked up her daughter. The little girl was obviously pretty sick, so she rushed to the doctor's office with her. It was en route to the doctor's office that she heard herself say to her little girl, "I just hope you don't have a fever, so you can go back to school. I have got to get back to work!" Thankfully, my friend did hear herself! She turned in her resignation, made some big material adjustments in her lifestyle and is very grateful that God has allowed her to see this choice.

The point is, for most of us there are options. We sometimes are in denial about them, but most of the time, they are there. The bare naked truth is that often we let the riches that are direct blessings from God, become obstacles in choosing the vocation to which he called us in Titus 2.

I read about one woman who saw the choice only when she began to look for child-care:

> My carefully worded advertisements for child-care literally came back to haunt me...I wanted someone who would encourage my children's creativity, take them on interesting outings, answer all their little questions, and rock them to sleep. I wanted someone who would be a "part of the family."
> Slowly, painfully, after really thinking about what I wanted for my children and rewriting advertisement after advertisement, I came to the stunning realization that the person I was looking for was right under my nose. I had been desperately trying to hire me (Dobson and Bauer, 135).

Connecting the dots

"But I thought this was a book about marriage; not parenting," you are thinking. What does all of this about *keepers at home* have to do with my marriage? I believe that our happiness in marriage is inextricably linked to our fulfillment of the roles God has assigned us in the home. In Titus two, the phrase *homemakers* is obviously included in a list of attributes for women that will make Christian homes stronger and happier. But, to me, the connections between good parenting and good marriage are all too obvious.

When we do parenting God's way, we are far more likely to experience the peace, harmony and faith-centered family living that God intends for us to know. Consistent discipline results in the *peaceable fruit of righteousness* (Hebrews 12:11). Just because a woman stays home with her kids doesn't mean she is a good disciplinarian, but the mother who leaves her children in day care certainly forfeits the consistency that's available when she *is* with her children throughout their days. Just because a woman stays home with her children doesn't mean that she is a good nurturer, but she certainly has more time for nurturing if she *wants* to nurture. Just because a woman stays home with her children doesn't mean she is wisely using that time to fill those little souls with the Word of God, but, unlike the mother who spends the majority of her waking hours away from her children, she *can* be wisely using the teachable moments. We just automatically give our children more spiritual insurance when we, as faithful moms, are with them more.

I realize that what I am saying is not popular. I realize that it is terribly old fashioned (as old as the Word). I realize that there are magazines out there that are totally devoted to salving the consciences of working moms. The articles in these publications bombard us with the reasons that giving the care of our children to others can actually be beneficial to our families. But anyone with a even a casual knowledge of God's Word and the spiritual responsibility that He has placed on parents throughout time, can see that the spiritual benefits and advantages (the ones that really matter) belong to those children who are spending their days with a mother who desperately wants to plant faith in their little hearts.

It is very difficult for me to conceive of the home in which both parents work full time outside the home, being a home where Deuteronomy 6:6,7 can possibly have a significant practical application.

> And these words which I command you today shall be in your heart.
> You shall teach them diligently to your children, and shall talk of them when you sit in your house, when you walk by the way, when you lie down, and when you rise up.

Yet God told His people of old that this is the way we transfer our faith to our children:

> ...that you may fear the Lord your God, to keep all His statutes and His commandments which I command you, you and your son and your grandson, all the days of your life, and that your days may be prolonged.
> (Deut. 6:2)

Having suggested that we are more likely to raise faithful children when we follow God's plan for parenting, let's ask some questions:

- Are there more stresses on my marriage if my children are disobedient and rebellious?

- Am I able to concentrate more on my relationship with my husband if I am less worried about my teenagers being with the wrong crowd or involved in dangerous behaviors?

- Can I have more times of peaceful communication with my husband if there is order and discipline in my home?

- Can my husband more confidently provide if I've been successful in guarding my children's hearts from materialism?

- Are there deep and eternal joys I can share with my husband in a way that brings us ever closer when we together watch our children become Christians and live victoriously?

These are rhetorical questions. Obviously our parenting affects our marriages. Following God's Will in one area of my life may very well produce benefits in another...sometimes priceless benefits when I least expect them. God's blessings are new every morning (Lam. 3:23).

What about switching roles?

The stay-at–home dad scenario is a two million strong (and growing) phenomenon in America today (Donaldson-Evans). It goes something like this: Cathy is a well paid attorney married to Tom, a smart, steady guy who loves the outdoors. He's a forest ranger. They want children and they don't want their children to be raised by strangers. Cathy's salary is twice Tom's (and besides, Cathy can't imagine her life without her career), so it only makes sense that Cathy continue working and Tom, who's so excited about this little boy who can romp in the woods with him, become the primary caregiver for Junior.

So what's wrong with that?

I believe that it is very difficult for a woman who is the breadwinner to be subject to her husband in all things. I believe it is more difficult to guide her house (I Timothy 5:14), and I believe she makes tremendous sacrifices of maternal blessings that come with being the primary care-giver. But it really doesn't matter what I think. Titus 2:5 makes it very clear that the career a Christian wife with children should pursue is that of keeper at home. Just as the injunction to be "obedient to their husbands" is not a reversible command, neither is the "keeper at home" command. The very strong conclusion of the verse (that the Word of God be not blasphemed) re-emphasizes that God is serious about these teachings for young Christian wives. Remember faith is choosing to do things His way in every area of our lives, even when human reasoning tempts us to make other choices.

The good news is...

Let me hasten to add that, even in the face of such dangerous trends, I am extremely encouraged that more and more young families in the church are making a conscious decision to keep Mom at home through the child rearing years. They are practicing life on one salary by banking the wife's salary during the years she works before having children. They are refraining from getting into a situation of debt that requires more take home pay than the husband can make. Young women are creatively finding income supplements that they can generate from home. They are making material sacrifices because their primary concern is the spiritual well being of their children.

Just this week, I got a call from a sister I've never met. She wanted to order copies of the parenting book *Your Mama Don't Dance* and explained that she uses them as baby shower gifts, the last one going to a mom in Birmingham, Alabama. She said this mom had read the book, taken a long, hard look at the choices she was making as a parent and made the decision to resign from her position at work and come home to be a full-time mom to her children. I don't know this mom. I do know that her children were given a gift this week that will impact their entire lives and eternities. As long as there are those who are willing to honestly examine the choices they are making, we will keep saying the obvious but unpopular truth: children whose moms choose to be at home with them are better off—physically, emotionally and spiritually. Our strength to keep teaching our teenagers God's will from Titus 2 is renewed when we see young families rejoicing in God's perfect plan for their homes. *Godliness with contentment is great gain* (I Tim. 6:6).

Think about it:

1. Why do you think women (rather than men) are specifically instructed to be the teachers of the "good things of Titus 2:3-5? Do you believe that older women are keeping this command to teach today? Why or why not?

2. How is it that the word of God is blasphemed when the commands of Titus 2 are ignored?

3. How can those of us who have daughters instill the principles of Titus 2 in their hearts while they are young? Give specific examples of activities we can do with them to prepare them to be characterized by the qualities listed in verses 3-5.

4. How can husbands encourage their wives to be keepers at home? Are there situations you could cite in which the wife wants to be a keeper at home, but is required to have another career by her husband? Give ideas about how this situation can be resolved.

5. Make a practical list of early decisions teens can make to better prepare them to have Titus 2 homes. Encourage those who have teens at home to share this list during an upcoming family devotional.

Blessings of Keeping

Keeping scrapbooks and photos and memories,
Keeping late hours as seamstress and maid,
Keeping up with appointments, schoolwork and chores,
Keeping guard when someone is afraid.

Keeping food in the pantry and gas in the car,
Keeping warranties, coupons, receipts,
Keeping bouquets of dandelions, locks of blonde hair,
Keeping score when the children compete.

Keeping tabs on where everyone's going,
Being sure that my cell phone is near.
Keeping sleeping bags stashed in my closet
For those friends who always end up here.

But mostly just keeping on keeping on,
For life's about sowing and reaping,
When one day my home finds a place at his throne
I'll praise him for blessings of keeping.

Cindy Colley

Works Cited:

Colley, Glenn and Cindy (revised 2004) Your Mama Don't Dance (Gurley, AL, Glenn and Cindy Colley, Gurley, AL)

Dobson, Dr. James C. and Bauer, Gary L. (1990) Children at Risk (Dallas, TX Baker Books)

Donaldson-Evans, Catherine (2002) Modern Mr. Moms Are Multiplying {On-line}, URL: http://www.foxnews.com/story/0,2933,6899,00.html.

Thayer, Joseph Henry D.D. (1977 Fourth Edition) Thayer Greek English Lexicon of the New Testament (Grand Rapids, MI, Baker Books)

CHAPTER EIGHT

Who's In Charge?

———————————— ♪ ————————————

What brings peace in the home? Your home wants peace, but what are its ingredients? The simple answer is making a Christ-centered home, and everyone fulfilling his or her family role. Get this wrong and you can kiss peace goodbye.

There are some things in the Bible that are easy for me to obey because they make perfectly good sense to me. There are other times when I obey despite the fact that my fleshly side would like to rebel. Do you find times when God's way doesn't exactly harmonize with how you'd do a thing?

This chapter is about a God-given key to musical marriage that may not make sense to a woman—or even to her husband, for that matter. It's the leadership role of the husband. Have you ever seen a home where the wife was a natural leader and the husband was clearly not a leader? Have you ever seen a home where both wanted to lead? We live in a time where you hear a cultural crash when you teach that a husband has authority over his wife. Our secular society finds this offensive.

The best way to grasp this law of God is to simply walk through the verses and read them. I will do that and make observations along the way.

Genesis 2

And the Lord God said, "*It is* not good that man should be alone; I will make him a helper comparable to him." Out of the ground the Lord God formed every beast of the field and every bird of the air, and brought *them* to Adam to see what he would call them. And whatever Adam called each living creature, that *was* its name. So Adam gave names to all cattle, to the birds of the air, and to every beast of the field. But for Adam there was not found a helper comparable to him. And the Lord God caused a deep sleep to fall on Adam, and he slept; and He took one of his ribs, and closed up the flesh in its place. Then the rib which the Lord God had taken from man He made into a woman, and He brought her to the man. And Adam said: "This *is* now bone of my bones And flesh of my flesh; She shall be called Woman, Because she was taken out of Man." Therefore a man shall leave his father and mother and be joined to his wife, and they shall become one flesh. And they were both naked, the man and his wife, and were not ashamed, (Gen. 2:18-25).

We get the first glimpse of the woman's role in the home with the very creation of Eve. She was made second, and for a special reason: helper and companion for the man.

She was different from him in so many ways, and each difference was deliberately and delicately prepared with the hand of God. He meant to make her different from man. Adam needed her. You might say she needed Adam too (who would deny that?), but that wasn't the point. She was made to help him.

Genesis 3

As Eve and then Adam placed the forbidden fruit to their lips and ate, human sin entered our world for the very first time. God had promised separation, called death, if they did this, and so it occurred. No more would our ancient grandparents enjoy the freedom of open joy and communication with the Almighty. Sin had divided them. And in this picture we have another problem which, sadly, Adam's sons after him have re-created over and over for generations.

Picture that first sin in your imagination. Picture the serpent, Eve, the tree, the fruit. Now, I want to ask a question: Where's Adam? For years I'd picture this with Adam no where in sight until after Eve's sin. Then called by his wife, he comes and also eats the fruit. But that's not what happened. Genesis three, verse six says "…when the woman saw that the tree *was* good for food, that it *was* pleasant to the eyes, and a tree desirable to make *one* wise, she took of its fruit and ate. She also gave to her husband with her, and he ate." He was with her. Why didn't he speak up? Why didn't he grab that sorry snake by the tail, twist him in a knot and send him sailing? Why didn't Adam take the lead in this spiritual situation and simply handle it? In the greatest leadership moment of his life, he failed.

A man is not like a woman. He thinks mostly in black and white, while his wife is more sensitive to the emotional nuances around her. Both are vital to marriage. Perhaps that's why the devil pursued Eve with this godless temptation instead of the man Adam. Maybe he knew that Eve would be more easily persuaded with words like

You will not surely die. For God knows that in the day you eat of it your eyes will be opened, and you will be **like God, knowing good** and evil.

So when the woman saw that the tree *was* good for food, that it *was* **pleasant** to the eyes, and a tree desirable to make *one* wise...(Gen. 3:4-6, emphasis added).

Why couldn't Eve be satisfied with the leadership of her God and her husband? Why was she so moved by an offer to be a little god? And why wasn't her husband the spiritual leader he should have been at that moment?

Adam's punishment was this:

Because you have heeded the voice of your wife, and have eaten from the tree of which I commanded you, saying, 'You shall not eat of it': "Cursed is the ground for your sake; In toil you shall eat of it All the days of your life. Both thorns and thistles it shall bring forth for you, And you shall eat the herb of the field. In the sweat of your face you shall eat bread Till you return to the ground, For out of it you were taken; For dust you are, And to dust you shall return (Gen. 3:17-19).

But Eve's punishment was unique, and while her daughters spanning all future generations do not bear the guilt of her sin, they nevertheless reap the consequences of her punishment: "I will greatly multiply your sorrow and your conception; In pain you shall bring forth children; Your desire *shall be* for your husband, And he shall rule over you" (Genesis 3:16). (Cindy believes that the sorrow in conception includes all the issues related to the reproductive system in women—including PMS, cycles, hormonal changes, etc.) The word "desire" in the Hebrew is *tesh-oo-kaw'* and, according to Strong's Lexicon, means "*stretching* out after; a *longing*: - desire."

> *Sometimes men are too concerned about football and fishing and hunting and trucks and sometimes they are lucky enough to have wives who long for spiritual leadership.*

Then it says of her relationship with Adam, "He shall rule over thee." This Hebrew word is *maw-shal'* and Strong's says it means, "...to have dominion, govern...reign, have power."

The New Testament maintains the husband-leadership principle in I Corinthians 11: 7-9 with these plain words:

For a man indeed ought not to cover *his* head, since he is the image and glory of God; but woman is the glory of man. For man is not from woman, but woman from man. Nor was man created for the woman, but woman for the man.

Again we are pointed back to the garden of Eden to understand this. The wife in her home has a God-given purpose which began some six thousand years ago. She was a helper, perfectly suited to her husband. He was not created for her; she was created for him. He was to be the leader in the home

Ephesians Five

Perhaps this is the strongest way to express the husband-leader role in marriage. Paul does something one would only do with God's permission, and he does it by inspiration. He compares the relationship Christ has with His church to the relationship a man has with his wife. In part, the passage says this:

Wives, submit to your own husbands, as to the Lord. For the husband is head of the wife, as also Christ is head of the church; and He is the Savior of the body. Therefore, just as the church is subject to Christ, so let the wives be to their own husbands in everything, (Eph. 5:22-24).

After considering the earlier passages, this is no surprise. It is merely consistent with the others. What is particularly interesting is the force with which God lays this out. Observe:
1. A wife is to submit to her husband as if she is serving the Lord.
2. A wife is to view her husband as the church should view Christ Jesus.
3. A wife is to be subject to her husband in everything.

I Peter 3:1-6

Wives, likewise, be submissive to your own husbands, that even if some do not obey the word, they, without a word, may be won by the conduct of their wives, when they observe your chaste conduct accompanied by fear. Do not let your adornment be merely outward—arranging the hair, wearing gold, or putting on fine apparel—rather let it be the hidden person of the heart, with the incorruptible beauty of a gentle and quiet spirit, which is very precious in the sight of God. For in this manner, in former times, the holy women who trusted in God also adorned them-selves, being submissive to their own husbands, as Sarah obeyed Abraham, calling him lord, whose daughters you are if you do good and are not afraid with any terror.

What makes this passage so poignant is the scenario: a believing wife married to an unbelieving husband who isn't interested in hearing God's word. This situation exists somewhere in most congregations of God's people today, and I've pointed many struggling Christian women to this great passage. "How can I convert him if he won't come to worship with me? He won't even let me talk to him about the Bible any more!" The answer Peter gives is to live before him as an humble child of God yourself, and be an obedient wife with a meek and quiet spirit. Be like Sarah who was submissive to Abraham, and called him "lord."

Cindy and I have talked a great deal about this chapter and how difficult this command is in a world where girls are reared to compete with men and seek equality in everything. Add to that the fact that so many women bring home a substantial part of the family's income, and a transformation often occurs. The wife gradually becomes an equal in authority in the marriage with her husband. This cultural climate has motivated many a Bible class teacher to soften the truth of God's word on the subject. Are you brave enough to accept it? Remember: Faith is not telling God what we want and patiently waiting for Him to give it to us. Faith comes by hearing His word and believing that He knows, better than we, what's best for us. I can think of no place in our lives where that is truer than in our marriages.

Men, listen. It is next to impossible for your wife to be what I have just described from God's word if you won't lead. In so many of the marriage seminars Cindy and I present there will be at least one or two women who say, "I want to be what the Scriptures say a wife should be to her husband. But my husband just won't lead. What can I do?" Sir, in such a case, you may be promoting sin in the life of your own family without realizing it. If you don't lead, she can't follow. Your children will grow to learn that the one with real authority and leadership in the home is not Dad, but Mom. As the Scriptures we have just read plainly teach, God will never be pleased with that. Reread these passages and ask yourself, "How can I improve in loving, godly leadership in my family?"

I think men need to know that they have authority and a duty to lead--especially spiritually. This is the dire need in so many homes where Christian women are desperately trying to raise faithful kids. These women need to be able to count on loving leadership regarding worship, activity in the congregation, home devotionals, and discipline of the children. There is a big chasm when looking for men who have any concern about any details of home leadership. This burden falls way too often on women. This is often true even in homes of preachers. The biggest thing my wife hears from faithful women is "I am tired of having to initiate the spiritual. Men are often good at initiating everything else but that."

Men need to be more like Zacharias who said firmly, "His name is John" (Lk. 1:63), and mean it, or more like Joseph who was constantly protective of Mary and Jesus, leading them where God wanted them to be even if it meant personal peril for him (Lk. 1, 2). Sometimes men are too concerned about football and fishing and hunting and trucks and sometimes they are lucky enough to have wives who long for spiritual leadership.

One wife wrote, "It's hard for us to submit sexually, financially, career-wise, domestic-wise, when there's nothing to submit to or feed on spiritually."

Get Practical
--The Time And Place

1. Men: Initiate prayer with your wife and family; at the supper table, at night, when you come upon a bad accident on the highway, when you get home from worship having heard the announcements about the sick, or when your friends are experiencing sorrow.

2. Men: Initiate family devotionals every night. Start early enough that the group isn't too sleepy to carry this out. Too sleepy means too cranky and thus the purpose is lost. Think about this ahead of time and say, "Everyone into the den. It's story time!" After the children are grown your Christian wife will treasure the time you spend together in Bible reflection and prayer. Cindy and I do this every night—sometimes reading a Bible-based book together, a chapter each night with discussion.

3. Men: Make sure you and your family are present for all the worship assemblies. Make sure your children grow up knowing that you are a dad who puts the Lord first above all else (Matt. 6:33).

4. Men: During the days, find spiritual meaning in God's cre-

ation and in daily activities. Let your wife and children know you are a man of God who meditates on His word. Be the kind of husband and father who will guide his family so that prayers will flourish and never be hindered.

5. Men: Take the role of husband seriously. When a dilemma arises, examine the facts, listen carefully to your wife's and children's input, then make a firm decision. Occasionally call a family meeting and require every family member's presence. This may be helpful in addressing a variety of issues: consistent tardiness on Sunday mornings, high power bills, disrespect for Mom, or stricter limits on television viewing. Conduct the meeting and guide your family in things that are right and good.

Think About It:

1. For the next week, make a list of spiritual initiatives in your home that are husband-initiated. At the end of the week, review the list and commit to making needed improvements.

2. How will your prayer lives together be hindered when the husband fails at spiritual leadership?

3. Is it right for women to lead devotionals at home when men fail to do so? Discuss.

4. In what ways can we help our daughters to find spiritual leaders to marry? How can they be identified prior to marriage?

5. List practical suggestions to aid husbands in developing spiritual leadership. Here's a start:
    a. Take your Bible to work and study during breaks.
    b. Take your son to visit and encourage members who are weak or unfaithful.
    c. Have the elders over for a meal. Learn from them.

Just Daddy

He's always there for the big times...
Recitals, big games, spelling bees;
He's so busy down at the office,
But still he can make time for these.

But I think it's the quiet "at home" times
That mean most to the children and me;
Times when the preacher's just "Daddy"...
The daddy no one else will see.

Just Daddy who shoots ball, pets kittens and laughs
At jokes he's heard over again;
Who pops corn for movies, builds toys in his shop,
Plays monopoly, but lets Mama win.

He stands up and cheers for them, kneels down and prays for
them,
Listens, laughs, loves and forgives;
While listening to the sermons he preaches of life
They're learning the way that he lives.

Cindy Colley

CHAPTER NINE

Intimacy
The Undefiled Bed

Neither of this book's authors are certified counselors or therapists in the area of sexual intimacy in marriage. But we have been married for twenty-seven years. Anyone else who's been married for that long can attest to the fact that experience is an exacting taskmaster in all areas of the marriage relationship. This part of married life is no exception. But most importantly, the writers do have God's word on the subject. So do you. It may surprise you to know that God's word has a lot to say about sex. In fact, there is more written about marital sex than about finances, prayer or communication as they specifically relate to marriage.

God has always been serious about the sacredness of sexual intimacy. Prayer is a grand blessing inside of marriage and outside of marriage. We enjoy God's material blessings as married people and as singles. The gospel invitation is open to people both inside and outside of marriage. But sexual intimacy is a blessing and responsibility that has always been reserved for marriage between a man and a woman. God has built this fence around intimacy because He made us and He knows what will bring us ultimate joy and fulfillment that is real. I believe that God's people can enjoy a richer and more meaningful sex life than anyone else on earth, because even as their flesh is one in the act of intimacy, their spirits are inseparably tied together in Christ. No relationship outside of Christ can match the depth of unity found in this dual physical and spiritual oneness.

As we've noted, there are four Greek words for our English word love. They are *phileo*, which is brotherly love or friendship love; *storge*, which is family love; *agape*, which is Christian love; and *eros*, which is physical love or sexual love. Have you ever thought about the fact that the marriage relationship is the only relationship in which we can express all four of these kinds of love? Agape, the love which loves *in spite of* rather than *because of* should characterize us in all relationships. Phileo and storge are kinds of love that are more specific. I love my shopping pal or my golfing buddy with both phileo and agape. I love my daddy with storge and agape and maybe even phileo. But it is only my spouse that I love with agape, storge, phileo and eros. I love him with agape when he is cross or ill with me. I love him with phileo when we are antiquing together. I love him with storge when we hold our baby for the first time. I love him with eros when we share that world of intimacy reserved for two in marriage. Where one love may temporarily be overcome by another, all of these loves are part of the dynamic of marriage at all times. Agape controls the other three loves, but they are all very powerful. The relationship with the one I've chosen for life truly becomes the most amazingly complex of all human relationships when, after the ceremony, the fourth love is added to the other three that have already been developing. Intimacy is the link that makes the circle complete. It is the physical expression (eros) of commitment (agape), friendship (phileo), and family (storge).

So how can I make this expression the best it can be?

The basic answer surfaces once again: anything is at its best when done God's way. And the basic rewards apply: submission to God in one area of marriage enhances all aspects of the marriage.

The first five verses of First Corinthians 7 hold several keys to sexual fulfillment in marriage:

> *Nevertheless, because of sexual immorality, let each man have his own wife, and let each woman have her own husband. Let the husband render to his wife the affection due her, and likewise also the wife to her husband. The wife does not have authority over her own body, but the husband does. And likewise the husband does not have authority over his own body, but the wife does. Do not deprive one another except with consent for a time, that you may give yourselves to fasting and prayer; and come together again so that Satan does not tempt you because of your lack of self-control. (1 Cor. 7:2-5)*

The Place for Sex

Here we find the place for sex is marriage. Notice verse two classifies all sex outside of marriage as fornication. Hebrews 13:4 adds that the marriage bed is pure while God will judge fornicators and adulterers. God's strategic placement of sex within marriage is for all generations and all cultures. Many diseases, countless deaths, and millions of abortions would be avoided if our culture respected God's placement of sex. Many children in our country whose hearts are bleeding would be whole if their parents respected God's will about sex. Our Father always knows what is best.

When we recognize God's place for sex and revere His will, it changes and impacts lots of areas of our lives. It changes the kinds of entertainment we enjoy, the way we dress, the way we talk to friends of the opposite sex. A reverence for God's will about sex helps mold our entire selves into conformity with His will.

Sexual Frequency

We also find within these verses God's rules for the frequency of sex. Verse 4 is, in practical terms, a restatement of the golden rule with a specific application for sex within marriage. God's rule for sexual frequency is simple: You have sex whenever either or both spouses want or need sexual fulfillment.

I can hear the groans of those, especially of the female gender who just read the above rule. "Give me a break," you may be saying. "Surely God doesn't expect me to be at this man's beck and call for his selfish satisfaction." Listen closely again.

The rule of I Corinthians 7:4 is a restatement of the golden rule as it applies to sex within marriage. *Both* spouses are operating under the golden rule. That means the satisfaction within the marriage bed is never selfish. It is always seeking the good of the other partner. The wife's goal in sexual intimacy is to fulfill her husband's needs and desires. Her husband's body belongs to her! So, as her prized possession, she is glad for the chance to take care of all of his needs and desires. The husband's goal is to make his wife as happy as she can be in the sexual relationship. He is responsive to her desires and always considerate of her physical and emotional condition. Both are respectful of the other above themselves.

Having said all of this, we must acknowledge that the needs of sexual intimacy are not always mutual. Husbands normally need frequent sex (key words: need and normally). God made men to need sexual fulfillment on a regular basis. The husband's need for sex is, in a real sense, like his hunger for food. After being intimate and fulfilled, the satisfaction allows him to happily focus on the important tasks of his days. But as time goes by, he needs to have that hunger satisfied again. If he isn't able to be intimate with his wife, he soon becomes easily distracted. His thoughts become increasingly consumed with his hunger. He becomes emotionally stressed and easily frustrated. Temptations to look and lust become more difficult to avoid in our undressed society. He *needs* sexual intimacy. This is not being oversexed. This is normal.

But wives are different. Mrs. M (M for married) can enjoy an enormous sexual high when intimate with her husband. She looks forward to being with him on such a personal level, exclusive from everyone else in the world. She enjoys thinking about sex with him and knowing that he is looking forward to their sexual times together. She especially loves the fact that he is constantly looking for ways to enhance the sexual experience for her--asking her what she most enjoys, trying new techniques (new to them, anyway), and just always working to make the sexual aspect of her life better and better.

But there is a big difference between a physical hunger--a metabolic urge that shouts after a period of time--and a longing anticipation. It is a difference that is perfectly designed by a creative Mastermind who knows what will make our relationships the best they can be. I would hate to think what our home would be like if both of us had the same physical urge for sex. When we had to be apart for a few days, we would become so stressed and consumed with this need that neither would have the clear thinking capacity to care for the children! I'd hate to think what life would be like if we were both on the emotional wavelength of the wife. We'd think a lot about having sex, put it on our lists, hope to get around to it, but our schedules would just be so cluttered that we'd rarely ever take the time for this awesome and very important bond of married life. God specifically designed our sexual psyches to complement each other. And then he made the rule: *The wife has not have authority over her own body, but the husband does* and visa versa. He went on to say, "Do not deprive one another...so that Satan does not tempt you because of your lack of self control."

There are, as we mentioned before, certain temptations that become very strong, especially for the man who has been deprived of sexual fulfillment. Visual temptations that might have formerly been relatively easy to overcome become increasingly difficult. As one man puts it, "The sexual volume just gets louder and louder in my head and I can't turn it down. I need a release."

The bottom line is that each partner has his/her own challenges in submitting sexually to the golden rule. It's difficult but I have to get into my spouse's brain and figure out what he/she needs and then happily comply. Sometimes it may be having sex when I am tired or out of the mood, because I'm in his brain and I know how he needs it. Sometimes it may be postponing sex when I really want it because I'm in her brain and I know that she is extremely exhausted or has the cramps. It's taking the golden rule to bed with us.

I believe that God's people can enjoy a richer and more meaningful sex life than anyone else on earth, because even as their flesh is one in the act of intimacy, their spirits are inseparably tied together in Christ.

"But you didn't tell us how often to have sex yet," you say. "Is it twice a week or three times a week, or what?" Well God didn't get that specific in the golden rule but I will give this piece of advice that's helped some couples I've known. I think it's a good idea to sit down and talk about needs and expectations. It may go something like this:

W. "Honey, do you think if we sort of plan to have sex every third night that you would be comfortable with that?"

H. "I think every other night would be better for me, unless there's a night when it's really difficult for you. Then, if you say something very nice to me, I think I could wait."

W. "Well, it sort of helps me to get the kids to bed and be in the right mood, if I know ahead of time what you are thinking."

H. "How 'bout if we shoot for every other night and then if there's a reason we need to postpone, we'll just do it?"

W. "But I kinda' like to be spontaneous, too. Do you think if we have a plan that it might take away all the fun of spontaneity?"

H. "Honey, you just be spontaneous all you want. I think I can handle spontaneous. Can you flex a little bit if I surprise you with a babysitter and roses?"

W. "I think I'm okay with that."

H. "Can we start this plan tonight?"

W. (With a wink) "We'll see how nice you are to me."

The golden rule is so big. It also encompasses mood, timing and technique. Agape rules eros. To agape my husband is to get into his psyche and seek to do what he enjoys most sexually. Agape means I do what is best for the other party even if there's nothing in it for me. What I do, then, if I agape my wife, is try to figure out what would most please her. Again...agape over eros.

Setting the Mood

So, if I'm a man, I've figured out that women need lots of emotion in the big sexual picture. If a man seems only interested in her when it's time for sex, then that sexual encounter will be less than satisfying. He may be thinking, "Well, haven't I shown her that I care by working hard all day down at the plant to provide this house and that SUV, etc...?" But, you see, a house and an SUV are not romantic. They are not emotional. But walking up behind her, swatting her on the bottom with a dish towel and saying, "Can I dry with the cutest dishwasher I've seen all day?"--that is thoughtful, romantic, sweet, and helpful. That makes the mood better later on. Men, we can figure this out.

And, if I'm a woman, I can figure out that men need to feel sexually appreciated. I can technically obey I Corinthians 7:5 by simply complying each time my husband asks for sex. But the trump command is the golden rule. If I haven't let the golden rule temper my compliance, then the greatest of sexual pleasures is out of my reach. My husband can surely tell the difference between that "Again, already?" look and that "Come and get me" wink. If wives make husbands feel that sex is a curse or a burden, it will ironically become such to both partners. If wives can let their husbands know on Tuesday morning that they will be looking forward to Tuesday night's rendezvous (a card, a note on his napkin, or an email), Tuesday will be a better day for both partners and the mood will be set for more satisfying sex. Ladies, we can figure this out.

Timing

It's interesting to notice the difference in questions asked by respective spouses. Women want to know if it's okay to request quick sex when husbands are sexually hungry, but wives are feeling like they've been run over by a giant truck called motherhood. Men ask, is it okay to request quick sex even when it's obvious that my wife is very tired? I believe the answer is yes...to both. I believe that both parties in such situations show consideration (agape) toward the other when they make the encounter brief. The husband's sexual need is temporarily met. The wife is given the gift of much needed rest. Both can go to sleep without feeling deprived. Sometimes this situation may play out in reverse. In either case, the outcome is the same if both parties are really considerate of the needs of one another.

Sometimes one partner may have crossed the line into complete and utter exhaustion, while the other party is in the mood for intimacy. When this occurs, and couples should try to make this a rare occurrence, don't deny your partner, but rather postpone. The words, "Oh honey, I promise if we can wait till tomorrow, I can make it worth the wait," have transformed many moments from disappointment to anticipation. I pick anticipation. You can figure this out, too.

Technique

The Bible has little to nothing to say about sexual technique; that is, the "how-to" specifics of sex. Some very good materials have been written by experienced therapists who base their recommendations on Biblical principles. I will include a couple of recommendations at the close of this chapter. It is important to remember that, within marriage, there is sexual freedom. Whatever is enjoyed by one or both partners without causing harm to either, can be part of this amazing intimate relationship. People often ask, for instance, if oral sex is a sin. Since your New

Testament does not address the matter, I believe it is not. When sexual activity includes both partners and both partners only, is not harmful to either partner in any way, and is desired by one or both partners, I believe God has granted us liberty in this undefiled bed of marriage.

I believe the most important contributor to technical sexual success is communication. Reading carefully chosen books about technique together helps overcome barriers about expressing desires to our partners. It makes us feel intimate and opens the door to communication about sex. Of course, books with crude language and/or immoral views about sex should be avoided. If, for instance, the author, while counseling heterosexual couples, is also counseling homosexuals about how to make their relation- ships more meaningful, he's probably not going to put your mar- riage on the fast track to spiritual success. His therapy will proba- bly not be golden-rule based.

Talking about sex preferences and learning to be comfortable with intimacy is, at least at first, much easier when you are com- menting on a chapter in a book. Many young married people were raised in homes in which sex was just not discussed at all. To sud- denly be comfortable with open discussion of intimacy is not on the radar. Reading together can be a big help.

But words are not the only important means of communication about sexual preferences. Sometimes just moving your spouse's hand a little during the actual sexual encounter to show your pref- erence is something to which your spouse will respond in an amazing way. You can affirm that you like what he/she is doing by your body language or even just by the way you are breathing. That's why it's called intimacy and that's why it's just for you two. That's why no therapist can tell you exactly how to do it. But if you are willing to stretch to communicate with each other about anxieties, preferences and ideas, you will find rewards in all areas of your marriage.

Warnings

Satan will make it easy for us, as children of God, to get off track sexually. He realizes that sexual deprivation, or selfish sex, or lust itself can destroy not only the sexual relationship, but the marriage and ultimately the lives of both the guilty and the inno- cent people in the household. He knows that the consequences of placing eros above agape is just another way of putting Christ in second place. He knows that the destruction and despair in the wake of sexual immorality is multi-generational and broad in its scope of ruin so he will put lots of temptations in the paths of Christian couples. He will make them attractive. They will not come with big yellow warning signs. He likes to make our homes chaotic so that the environment is not conducive for fulfilling intimacy. He likes to distract our minds from God's plan for our enjoyment of sex. Let's think of a few of his distractions. You can add to this list.

Pornography
Immodesty
Masturbation
Separations
Lack of discipline in the home
Immorality in entertainment
Invasive time demands from the workplace

In this, as in all areas of Christian living, doing it God's way is not always easiest. The distractions and interferences will be many. The rewards will be greater than you can imagine when both partners are seeking to give the sexual relationship of their marriage the protected and sacred place given it by its amazing Originator.

Think About It:

1. Have class members compose lists from Scripture of occasions when God commanded that sex be reserved for marriage. Discuss God's emphasis on this principle compared with today's relaxed attitude toward casual sex.

2. Have class members bring news articles to class demonstrating the chaos that ensues when society ignores God's will regarding sex. The lesson that God's restrictions are for our ultimate benefit can be seen daily in the newspaper.

3. Have spouses commit to pray together daily for the next week that their sexual relationship will be what God wants it to be and that, through fulfilling God's will in this area of marriage, other areas of golden rule application within the home will be positively affected.

4. If there are good Christian marriage counselors in your congregation or in your area, make sure the contact information for these is available to all class members. Great caution should be used by the class leaders in recommending counselors, however, since many are unconcerned about counseling in a Biblical context. Salvaging a human relationship while losing your soul is not a good bargain!

5. Look at I Peter 3:7. If husbands attempt to understand their wives' sexual needs and respond to them, is that a part of "dwelling with them according to knowledge"? Is there a connection between the effectiveness of prayer and the husband's desire to "know" his wife better?

Books that might help:

The Gift of Sex, by Clifford and Joyce Penner, Word Publishing

The Act of Marriage, by Tim and Beverly Lahaye, Zondervan

(Does not imply author endorsement of all materials contained in these books.)

Rules For PMS

(Since the beginning of PMS is admittedly sometimes unpredictable, some of these may be difficult to accomplish.)

A. Husbands

1. During this time, avoid the desire to resolve issues.
2. During this time, let her be the one to initiate intimacy, not you.
3. During this time, try to ease her workload.
4. Do not minimize your faults in the temptation to blame all problems on PMS. Sort through her criticisms and look for ways you really can improve.
5. Give her time away from children.
6. Pray about this.

B. Wives

1. Be aware that PMS is not a license to sin. It is a physical change producing an emotional change which creates a temptation to sin.
2. Try to become aware of its presence. Mark your calendar for when to expect this difficult time. You may not recognize it otherwise.
3. Tell your husband that difficult moments are coming for you.
4. Seek a physician's help if the problem is severe. Some medications may help.
5. Pray about this.
6. Exercise all month, and especially during these days. It will help you work out the frustrations.
7. Stay in God's book.
8. Be extremely careful not to let PMS make you abusive or violent toward your children or husband.

Don'ts:

1. Don't make important decisions during this time.
2. Don't over-schedule yourself during this time.
3. Don't consume excessive caffeine.
4. Don't express things you really can't stand about your husband; wait five days to address them. Don't express those things to anyone at this time—except the Lord.

CHAPTER TEN

Men: Fear This

———————— ♪ ————————

Several times during our marriage I have searched through my memory trying to recall the first time I laid eyes on Cindy. We were both freshmen at Freed-Hardeman University. Was there a moment—there must have been—when I looked at her the first time and said, "Hi, I'm Glenn," and she smiled that gentle smile of hers and said, "I'm Cindy." ? I definitely remember our first date. I was traveling with other male students to a small congregation on a Sunday to lead the worship and I was the song leader. At the last minute the others decided to invite dates and, since I didn't have a steady girlfriend, I went to the cafeteria to see who was eating that day. I saw Cindy in line and my friend, who was assisting me in this girl shopping (O.K. I didn't say I was particularly proud of it), said, "Hey, what about Cindy Holder?" Being in line she was somewhat confined and I seized the opportunity that launched the two of us into life together.

I've got a lot invested in this marriage, and I fully expect it to be my only one. We've built something, without really thinking too much about it in the weeks and months. It's a relationship that can only come with twenty-seven years of sharing the same car, bed, children, and supper table together. My union with her, to a great extent, has come to define who I am. I'm Cindy's husband. To think of taking actions that would devastate her and destroy our home is plainly unthinkable to me and, I hope, unthinkable to you in your marriage.

But the devil is the original home breaker. Every bitter discovery of adultery and all the rivers of tears and all the children of broken homes have wielded a sickening laugh from the prince of darkness. Perhaps his passionate motivation is to hurt God and the best way to do that is to hurt and destroy people. I don't know. But I know he is good at what he does and has been astonishingly successful. This chapter is designed to arm you for the fight against the devil himself and protect your marriage. I recommend you approach it with prayer and a commitment to change whatever you learn is giving the devil any advantage over you or making you susceptible to his devices. "Resist the devil and he will flee from you" (Ja. 4:7). "...nor give place to the devil" (Eph. 4:27).

If you want to safeguard your marriage from adultery, you must remember five key things revealed by God in one little chapter of the Great Book:

You Must Listen To The Right Teacher.

My son, pay attention to my wisdom; Lend your ear to my understanding, That you may preserve discretion, And your lips may keep knowledge" (Prov. 5:1-2).

How would you define wisdom? Wisdom is the ability to see how a particular course of action will turn out. Imagine a teenager, wrestling with the decision to accept or decline her boyfriend's proposal of matrimony, finding a quiet time with a grandfather to see what he thinks about it. What is she really asking as she seeks his wisdom? She is asking him to look into the crystal ball of his years of experience to predict the consequence of either decision. That's a matter of wisdom. This passage begins with a father saying in essence, "I know what will happen if you don't resist the temptation to commit sexual sin. Now bring me your ear. I want you to hear this clearly."

It frightens me to think of the places where today's kids learn sexual values. From friends? Maybe from humanistic universities? Perhaps even worse from the examples of Hollywood starlets or television talk-show hosts? Not to mention ill-informed parents. This chapter, inspired of the true God, is couched in the warm, practical setting of a father advising his son, and is here for us to read and internalize.

You Must Know How the Devil Works To Trap You In Sexual Sin

"For the lips of an immoral woman drip honey, And her mouth is smoother than oil; But in the end she is bitter as wormwood, sharp as a two-edged sword. Her feet go down to death, Her steps lay hold of hell" (Prov. 5:3-5).

The Devil never goes fishing without bait. And he's smart. He doesn't use things to entice us that we quickly and obviously view as bad, but rather offers us things which have, in some ways, appropriate uses. For a man to have a deep and intimate relationship with a woman is a good thing to be desired. In fact, God put it in our hearts to want this. But the Devil takes that desire and perverts it. He misappropriates it. Here's the progression:

a. He makes this whole matter seem innocent enough. Her lips are like honey. She is so sweet and he likes talking to her and being around her. He reasons, "What's the harm? We're just good friends. Nothing more." Adultery doesn't begin in the bedroom. It begins in benign places with benign conversations that over time increase into electric conversations. And it starts with sweet lips. As one adulterous husband said to me about his mistress not long before his wife divorced him, "How can anything so wonderful be this wrong?"

b. He uses flattery. "Her mouth is smoother than oil." Oil rubbed on strained, tense shoulders feels good and soothes us. Words of flattery stroke us that way, and men are often more susceptible to this than women. A man has a way of turning to pudding around a pretty woman who tells him how wonderful he is. He'll find himself hearing her words and seeing her expression when she's no longer in sight. We men want women to believe we are wonderful and to respect us. Wives whose husbands commit adultery are sometimes shocked to discover that the *other* woman isn't necessarily more physically beautiful than she. The home wrecker may be a little overweight, maybe shows very little interest in fashionable dressing, but she has something that caught that husband's attention. The King James translation calls it flattery in the next chapter, "For the commandment *is* a lamp; and the law *is* light; and reproofs of instruction are the way of life: To keep thee from the evil woman, from the flattery of the tongue of a strange woman" (Prov. 6:23-24). Did you get that, sir? It says that if you don't want to fall prey to the flattery of a woman who will destroy your family and your soul, you've got to stay in the Bible. Charge up on it every day. The word of God echoing in your ears will help you see unhealthy flattery when you hear it.

Let me make a suggestion. Any time a woman says something that makes you feel uncomfortable—such as personal flattery—always immediately say something about your wife. If you're at work and your female co-worker says, "M-m-m-m, you smell good today," say, "Thanks. My wife gave me this cologne and it's her favorite scent." When Potiphar's wife tried to seduce Joseph in Genesis 39, Joseph immediately pulled her husband into the conversation.

"And after a time his master's wife cast her eyes on Joseph and said, 'Lie with me.' But he refused and said to his master's wife, "Behold, because of me my master has no concern about anything in the house, and he has put everything that he has in my charge. He is not greater in this house than I am, nor has he kept back anything from me except yourself, because you are his wife. How then can I do this great wickedness and sin against God?" (Gen. 39:7-9 ESV).

Be aware of your male weaknesses, and remember that the Devil will do all he can to exploit them.

c. He destroys you with this woman. The end of this little adventure is never going to be sweet like it began. It will be bitter. "Her feet go down to death; her steps take hold on hell". She may not know it herself, but that's where she is leading this man. Death. Death to youth, death to joy of family, death to intimacy with his wife, death to innocence, death to a clean conscience, death to a good influence on his children. This instant heaven she offers at the beginning can quickly become an eternal hell.

You Must Know The Adultery Avoidance Secret So Well You Can Recite It In Your Sleep.

"Remove your way far from her, And do not go near the door of her house" (Prov. 5:8).

Here's the secret. You want to never, ever, ever be guilty of adultery? Then never, ever deliberately go around a woman to whom you feel attracted, or who, in one way or another, is trying to sexually attract you. Remember this: Adultery typically begins in innocent places and in small ways; a lingering glance; a statement that can be taken two ways. The devil takes the threads of flirtation and tries to weave them into a chain of bondage.

I'm a third generation preacher, and as such, was taught *The Rules* about preachers and women ever since I was old enough to understand. Maybe some of these will help you to see this point.

1. Limit your touching. A short pat on the back, a shake of the hand, a respectful hug, and that's all. Don't be touchy.

2. Never visit a woman alone in her home. This rule of course applies to any woman about whom a question might arise (not the 87 year old ailing widow). I have a good friend who committed adultery several years ago—a sinful affair which began with stopping by her house in his job to fill her propane tank. If he had declined to come into the house, his marriage and life would have been spared this devastation.

...the devil is the original home breaker. Every bitter discovery of adultery and all the rivers of tears and all the children of broken homes have wielded a sickening laugh from the prince of darkness

3. Never discuss detailed sexual problems with another woman. You don't need to hear her talk about those things. Satan will plant seeds and do all he can to cultivate them. When a woman raises such matters, you say, "I understand those are legitimate concerns, but I think it would be better if you discussed that with my wife. She's a faithful Christian and will advise you well."

4. Never go to lunch alone with a woman.

5. Don't experiment with pornography. Period.

It would be interesting to know how many of the Christian men over the last twenty years who became adulterers also had a habit of viewing pornography. Porn is a narcotic of the mind. It is addictive and mind-altering. It will affect the way a man views women and people in general. The problem often is that Christian men believe that since they are walking in Christ's light, a little viewing of pornography will be harmless. They may rationalize that they need to know what this is all about in order to talk intelligently and help others who have a problem with it. They may just view it as a victimless, harmless, private pastime. Read this verse again and apply it to the unclothed women of the internet. If you really want to protect your family from the man of sin that you can become, stay away from pornography altogether. Putting those images in your mind is like putting a rattlesnake in your pocket and thinking that since you were nice to him, he won't bite you. Don't go near the door of her house.

You must remember that adultery never turns out good.

Here are the five bullets the Devil has with your name on them when you're about to step into the world of sexual sin. He has no hesitancy in firing at you.

1. You'll risk losing the good things in life to someone else.
"Lest you give your honor to others, And your years to the cruel *one*; Lest aliens be filled with your wealth, And your labors *go* to the house of a foreigner" (Prov. 5:9-10).
A country song a few years back pictured a divorced husband driving past his old house and he moaned that it was his wife, his kids, his dog, his house, but not his truck.

2. You'll risk an STD.
"And thou mourn at the last, when thy flesh and thy body are consumed" *(Prov. 5:11).*

One woman we know learned of her husband's adultery when she had some physical symptoms that prompted a visit to the doctor. He ran tests and concluded she had a sexually transmitted disease. She shook her head and said, "That's not possible. I've not been with any man in my life except my husband." Then it hit her. She knew. She was carrying the disease of his sinful actions. Divorce soon followed.

3. You'll risk deep, gut-wrenching guilt.
"And say: 'How I have hated instruction, and my heart despised correction! I have not obeyed the voice of my teachers, nor inclined my ear to those who instructed me! I was on the verge of total ruin, in the midst of the assembly and congregation!'" *(Prov. 5:12-14).*

People sometimes remark after hearing me preach, "You really stepped on my toes today, Preacher." It's usually said in a teasing way, but this is serious. How would you like to have this awful sin to think about every time you hear preaching about God's love and Christ's sacrifice for our sin? How would you like to eat the Lord's supper in worship and be able to think of only one thing when examining your heart (I Cor. 11:28)?

4. You'll risk your eternity in heaven.
"For the ways of man *are* before the eyes of the Lord, and He ponders all his paths" (Prov. 5:21).

Adultery is not a rose that adorns the bosom, it's a dagger in the heart. The world can disagree and shake its fist at heaven, but Heaven won't relent. God isn't a liar, and what He said will be preserved for all generations to hear:

> Now the works of the flesh are evident, which are: adultery, fornication, uncleanness, lewdness, idolatry, sorcery, hatred, contentions, jealousies, outbursts of wrath, selfish ambitions, dissensions, heresies, envy, murders, drunkenness, revelries, and the like; of which I tell you beforehand, just as I also told *you* in time past, that those who practice such things will not inherit the kingdom of God. (Gal. 5:19-20)

5. You'll risk entrapment so complicated and strong that you never overcome it.

"His own iniquities entrap the wicked *man*, And he is caught in the cords of his sin. He shall die for lack of instruction, and in the greatness of his folly he shall go astray" (Prov. 5:22-23).

I sat on a porch one day with a man who had committed adultery. His wife had taken their children to the evening worship and had told him she was staying for the youth activity that followed. Before the activity she realized she had forgotten some awards their children had won that she was supposed to bring, and she dashed home alone to get them. She entered the house, saw a woman's purse on the sofa, bounded upstairs, and found her husband in bed with another woman. She quickly filed for divorce.

He said between sobs, "It was so stupid. I don't even love that woman. She means nothing to me. Now my wife is divorcing me and taking our children away from me. What am I going to do? I can't stand to lose her! If I could only turn back the clock!" I advised that if he would become a faithful Christian, over time he might regain her respect and she might then be willing to reconcile. He agreed, and vowed to me he would do just that. He was baptized into Christ. He left that day, and forty-eight hours later he was in the arms of the other woman again. How do you explain that? It was as this verse says. He was being held with the ropes of his sin. He didn't realize it, but when he first made love to that woman he gave up a great amount of future resolve to resist sin. Now he is, to some obvious degree, hooked. How far into this dark sin do you think he can go before he's to the point of no return?

You Must Focus On What You Have And Work To Make It Better.

When our son Caleb was in high school he got a job writing sports for our little local newspaper. He eventually possessed a press pass (and one for his dad) and we were visiting the locker rooms of professional basketball teams. (I've been kicked by Shaq while I was sitting under the basket with a camera, but I resisted the temptation to kick him back). Those athletes are impressive. They are lean and strong, tall and poised. They are richer than they've ever dreamed. And many of them enjoy attracting and bedding women in the various cities they play. You may think I'm crazy, and I really enjoyed watching their talents on the basketball court, but the fact is, I wouldn't trade places with any of them. Those sexual "players" have sex, but not love; women, but not devoted wives; relationships but not great marriages; money, but not fulfillment. Let me say it plainly: With reference to the total relationship a man can have and enjoy with a woman, God has saved His very best for Christians! The best life you can have with a woman is simple and sounds old fashioned and cross-grain to our modern culture, but it's true. The best is abstinence before marriage and monogamy in marriage--one man for one woman. You learn about intimacy in each other's arms. You explore the joys God has made possible with one another in a context of full commitment and trust. You sleep with the one who will be there for you when you are old and cannot care for yourself. Listen to the inspired words of Solomon:

Drink water from your own cistern, And running water from your own well. Should your fountains be dispersed abroad, Streams of water in the streets? Let them be only your own, And not for strangers with you. Let your fountain be blessed, And rejoice with the wife of your youth. *As a* **loving deer and a graceful doe, Let her breasts satisfy you at all times; And always be enraptured with her love.**
(Prov. 5:15-19)

Can a marriage survive adultery? In some cases it can, but be prepared for a rocky road. The guilty party should resolve himself (or herself) to this reality: Since you broke the trust once, your spouse will be haunted, for a long time, by the possibility that you'll break it again. So, swallow hard and humbly accept whatever your spouse needs to develop that trust again. A wife whose husband has been unfaithful wants him to change jobs if the other woman is at his workplace. She wants full access to his phone, his computer, his passwords, his pockets, and his wallet. She wants the freedom to walk into his work to say hello at any time. You get the idea. Any resistance to this total accountability will immediately make the innocent party assume the worst.

Tonight before you sleep, thank God for the wife of your youth. Hold her close, never let her, or you, go.

Think about it:

1. Why do you think God made men with a need for frequent sex? What would happen to young marriages if this was suddenly and permanently gone?

2. What were the consequences of adultery in David's life?

3. Without using names, cite instances of people you know who have chosen to commit adultery and observe how accurate Proverbs five is in predicting adultery's heartaches even today.

4. Under what circumstances would you encourage a friend to stay in a marriage where his or her mate has committed adultery?

5. Jesus said that it is possible for someone to treat his spouse in such a way as to "cause" her to commit adultery. Read Matthew 5:32. What is the circumstance Jesus gives? Are there other similar circumstances? Is Jesus saying that a husband or wife is ever justified in committing adultery or merely that he/she is pushed in that direction by the actions of the spouse?

6. What precautions are in place in your marriage right now that have prevented both of you from adultery?

7. Discuss computer and television safeguards that can be taken to keep your home pornography free.

It's A Jungle Out There!

Be ready. Be watchful. Be prayerful. Beware!
Be always on guard. Be careful! He's there.
He stalks like a lion, his prey to ensnare.
He's the king of the darkness in his jungle out there.

If he made a loud roar, you would know he's around,
But he creeps up behind, without making a sound.
Then with cords of worldly wisdom that seem so profound
He entraps you while you're sleeping. You don't even know you're bound.

That's the saddest thing about those cords that hold you in his power.
You're doomed and you don't realize the lateness of the hour.
You've grown to love his jungle. To his plans your will has cowered.
You don't know that you're the prey and in the end you'll be devoured!

So you learn the jungle lingo and you dance the jungle dance.
You swing like Tarzan, dress like Jane, and when you get the chance
You spread the jungle borders, binding others who were free,
And everything the lion wills is what you want to be.

Are you happy in the jungle? You would always answer "Yes.
I am doing what I love to do. This free life is the best!"
But your jungle is a doomed domain and with your king you're damned.
For the lion's long been conquered by the meek and mighty Lamb.

Cindy Colley

CHAPTER ELEVEN

Women: Bring Back the Stigma!

In a world in which "experts" have told us that adultery can actually be healthy for our marriages and in which Hollywood's icons trade partners more casually than they trade cars, our view of adultery can scarcely be unaffected. We have, even in the kingdom, adopted a tolerant view of broken marriage vows. I know of a congregation in which former spouses worship together along with the adulterer who caused the break-up of their marriage. Something is terribly wrong with this picture! God does not have a laissez-faire attitude about adultery! I pray as I write this that every reader will examine the following verses and be stricken with the hatred God has for adultery and its devastating consequences. May we hate what God hates. May we bring the lost stigma back into our families and into the hearts of our children. May the thought of my personally committing adultery scare me to death!...Or scare me to life as far from that sin as I can possibly live!

> The man who commits adultery with *another* man's wife, *he* who commits adultery with his neighbor's wife, the adulterer and the adulteress, shall surely be put to death, (Lev 20:10).

> Whoever commits adultery with a woman lacks understanding; He *who* does so destroys his own soul, (Prov. 6:32).

> Also I have seen a horrible thing in the prophets of Jerusalem: They commit adultery and walk in lies; They also strengthen the hands of evildoers, So that no one turns back from his wickedness. All of them are like Sodom to Me, And her inhabitants like Gomorrah, (Jer. 23:14).

> And because of them a curse shall be taken up by all the captivity of Judah who *are* in Babylon, saying, "The LORD

make you like Zedekiah and Ahab, whom the king of
Babylon roasted in the fire" because they have done dis-
graceful things in Israel, have committed adultery with their
neighbors' wives, and have spoken lying words in My name,
which I have not commanded them. Indeed I know, and *am* a
witness, says the Lord, (Jer 29:22-23).

By swearing and lying, Killing and stealing and committing
adultery, They break all restraint, With bloodshed upon
bloodshed. Therefore the land will mourn; And everyone
who dwells there will waste away With the beasts of the field
And the birds of the air; Even the fish of the sea will be
taken away, (Hos. 4:2-3).

You have heard that it was said to those of old, You shall not
commit adultery.' But I say to you that whoever looks at a
woman to lust for her has already committed adultery with
her in his heart, (Mat 5:27 -28).

But I say to you that whoever divorces his wife for any reason except sexual immorality causes her to commit adultery;
and whoever marries a woman who is divorced commits
adultery, (Matt. 5:32).

So He said to them, Whoever divorces his wife and marries
another commits adultery against her. And if a woman
divorces her husband and marries another, she commits adultery, (Mk. 10:11-12).

Whoever divorces his wife and marries another commits
adultery; and whoever marries her who is divorced from *her*
husband commits adultery, (Lk.16:18).

Now the works of the flesh are evident, which are: adultery,
fornication, uncleanness, lewdness, idolatry, sorcery, hatred,
contentions, jealousies, outbursts of wrath, selfish ambitions,
dissensions, heresies, envy, murders, drunkenness, revelries,
and the like; of which I tell you beforehand, just as I also
told *you* in time past, that those who practice such things will
not inherit the kingdom of God, (Gal. 5:19-21).

...having eyes full of adultery and that cannot cease from sin, enticing unstable souls. *They have* a heart trained in covetous practices, *and are* accursed children. They have forsaken the right way and gone astray, following the way of Balaam the *son* of Beor, who loved the wages of unrighteousness; (II Pet. 2:14-15).

Indeed I will cast her into a sickbed, and those who commit adultery with her into great tribulation, unless they repent of their deeds, (Rev. 2:22).

So what else is new?

Hopefully most readers at this point are thinking "She hasn't told me anything new about adultery yet." If you've persevered through a God-centered marriage book all the way to chapter eleven, you likely have strong convictions about protecting your marriage from adultery. The problem is that we live in a society that is subtly conducive to adultery. There are certain societal changes that have occurred within the last five decades that actually lend themselves to an adultery filled world around us. What are some of these changes and how can we build fences to keep these changes from threatening the security of our marriages?

Women in the Workplace

Recent statistics show that about 60% of women over the age of 16 are either employed or actively seeking employment. The female sector comprises about 46% of the U.S. labor force (U.S. Department of Labor). Also significant, from our vantage point, is the kinds of work women are doing today. In the fifties, women were typically working in fields with other women and children. Many were schoolteachers and nurses. A large segment of those workers were also secretaries, working in offices with men, but generally finding themselves in different social circles from their higher paid bosses. Today, lots more women are working in high paying, even high tech arenas. My friends work long hours, side by side with men, as computer programmers, aerospace engineers and medical professionals. They are actually in the presence of the men with whom they work for the majority of their waking hours.

This chapter is not to discuss the effects of feminism on the economy or even on society in general. This is about protecting our homes from adultery. However we slice it, this evolution in the gender picture at work has profoundly and negatively affected the strength of the American family. When a woman works closely with a person of the opposite sex for more hours each day than she sees her husband, it only takes a little chemistry for temptation to rear its ugly head at work.

Let me begin by stating an unpopular, but obvious truth. Our homes are better off, particularly when the children are growing up, with Mom at home. I do not see how we can apply the eternal principles of Deuteronomy 6:4-8 (all day long teaching) when we have our children for only about a third of their waking hours and into these hours we are trying to cram all of the chores, shopping, cooking, dinner and any extra-curricular activities. I think Titus 2:3-5 clearly teaches that the most important career of a Christian woman is to be a home-keeper. I believe it's a stretch to think we can work forty hours a week and have enough left of ourselves to joyfully keep and protect our homes physically, emotionally and spiritually. I think we have to journey away from God's Will and into the culture of our day to convince ourselves that it's a good plan for mothers to place their children's souls in the care of others day after day.

Having said all of that, let me hasten to add that I have seen desperate situations in which mothers had to be in the workplace. For those mothers who truly find no alternative, I offer my support and prayers. May God help you in this and every decision to provide for and protect those little souls that are dependent on you.

So what precautions should working women take to guard their marriages from adultery? First, it's important to remember that adultery doesn't begin in the bedroom. It begins in the boardroom, the office, on the ball field, or at the mall. It doesn't begin with intimacy. It begins with a look, a comment, a conversation, or a hug. Satan can get us incrementally when he can't get us all at once.

So here are some terribly antiquated rules to follow to safeguard an institution that is as old as the Garden of Eden. (Remember God's Word is very old!)

1. Avoid being alone with any man. If you make this a general rule of thumb that applies to all men of all ages, you won't have to deal with any claims that you are prejudiced or just don't like certain men. Work in areas where there are lots of people. If you have to go to a private room, keep the door open.

2. Don't go to lunch alone with a man. No exceptions.

3. Be accessible by phone and/or email to your spouse at all times of the day.

4. Don't ever share relational problems you may be experiencing at home with a man at work.

> *May we hate what God hates. May we bring the lost stigma back into our families and into the hearts of our children. May the thought of my personally committing adultery scare me to death!... Or scare me to life as far from that sin as I can possibly live!*

5. Don't flirt or participate in electric conversations. People at work talk about ridiculously personal things (the way someone's bottom is showing as she gestures at the plans spread out on the table, the frequency with which a woman has to go to the bathroom, the way a man's pants are unzipped, etc...) Avoid personal conversations. When you begin to feel that lines of discretion are being crossed, change the subject. If you feel that someone is flirting, say something about your spouse. (This works every time.)

6. If you ever feel a physical attraction or "chemistry" with a person of the opposite sex, get yourself immediately out of the situation (change projects, change jobs, ask for a transfer, etc.) Do what Joseph Genesis 39:13. Never put your marriage at risk.

7. Share details of your day openly and honestly each evening with your spouse. Never lie to your spouse about anything. Every totally honest day you spend with your spouse strengthens the barriers you are erecting against adultery.

8. Speak often and glowingly about your spouse when you are at work.

9. Whenever possible, avoid taking assignments that will take you out of town for lengthy periods of time without your husband.

10. Avoid projects that demand lots of overtime, especially projects that would keep you apart at bedtime.

The Internet

You don't need statistics to know I'm accurate in telling you that internet relationships are a serious threat to our marriages in the twenty-first century. I can tell you from just observing people I thought I knew quite well and from watching these people wreck and ruin innocent lives, that when we begin spending seemingly innocent private time on the computer, the anonymous relationships we form in a chat rooms and on web sites can turn into spiritually deadly trysts in the bedroom. I learned that my friend Janice, after twenty years of marriage to a faithful gospel preacher, had left behind her husband and two teenage children to travel across the country and move in with a man she met in a chat room. I learned that my friend Sam, was losing his job as a gospel preacher because his computer pornography addiction had led to physical acts involving women in the church. I learned that my friend Mary Ann had walked in on her husband…again…as he closed the door to his home office and nurtured his perverse pornography habit to the neglect of his three young children and his beautiful and dutiful Christian wife. I learned that my friend Dara recently discovered the "other" life her husband had been living for the past 15 years. Tim, Dara's husband, was a computer programmer. His own personal computer, when finally examined after one slip-up let his wife know there was an infidelity problem, revealed a long and deceptively sordid tale of pornography addiction and repeated liaisons with women even as he served their congregation as one of its ministers. Many counseling situations have found me sitting across the table from a wife whose world has just collapsed because of behavior triggered by internet misuse. It used to take a lot of rather bold immoral behavior to engage in conversation and liaisons that might escalate to an affair, but now that behavior is easily concealed and solicited by lonely people in chat rooms and on instant messaging services in your most private world. Pornography formerly required going into a store and purchasing magazines or going to an adult movie store for a rental. At least there was a deterrent there for one who was at all concerned about reputation. But the devil now peddles pornography in private perverted sanctuaries. He has successfully removed the stigma and he loves it when we step on the path to ruin thinking "No one will ever know".

So what can women do?

- Keep computers in open and busy places in your home.

- Purchase internet guards that are reliable in blocking pornographic material from your computer.

- Stay out of chat rooms in which you talk to people of the opposite sex that you don't know.

- Don't get on the computer at night after your husband goes to bed. Go to bed with your husband.

- Use your email server's blocking service to automatically delete emails that have sexual content. Most servers have the ability to delete emails that contain certain words. I have blocked all emails with headings containing the words breasts, Viagra, sexy, sex, fantasy (and lots more that I won't include here). This is a simple step to take, but your email content will be much less provocative if you do this at the outset.

- When suggestive emails do get by your guards, hit "delete". Never open questionable emails from people you don't know. If you accidentally delete an email you needed, the sender will find another way to contact you. Take precautions. Sometimes one click can put an image in your mind that you can't easily erase.

• If you already have a problem with pornography, quit cold turkey. Any attempt to wean yourself away from this temptation is merely feeding the addiction. If after quitting, you have a relapse (even one time), then set up an accountability system by which you will report to a responsible person daily. Tell someone outside of your family about the problem. Choose someone you respect. Then set up a daily communication system with this person, so you know everyday that you are committed to honestly "coming clean" with him/her about your addiction. If you still have relapses, seek professional Christian counseling and therapy.

• Stay away from www.myspace.com. This popular social utility remains largely unprotected from pornographers and sexual predators.

• Always err on the side of caution. If you veer into an area of internet use that makes you uncomfortable, whether it is a web site or a conversation via internet, just click away. Just as surely as you are always a click away from temptation, you are always a click away from safety. Just remember that the devil works very subtly. What is fun and interesting and just a little risqué, can lure you into deeper waters. The temptation to do something you never dreamed of doing doesn't appear with sirens and warning signals on your screen. It happens in a slow progression and you're suddenly more intimately and deeply involved than you ever could have imagined.

• If thy computer offend thee, cut it off (Matthew 5:30). If you find your computer is a negative obsession or a constant temptation and you just can't overcome it, then get rid of it. If you have to change jobs to get away from it, change jobs. Whatever sacrifice it takes to preserve your marriage and insure your salvation is a small price for eternity in heaven. I'd rather be totally illiterate in heaven than be the most computer savvy woman in hell.

Television and the Movies

Let me just simply state the object of this segment of the book: All Christians should eliminate most current network television and most current movies from their lives. This decision may seem radical and over-reactive to you at first. Let's think soberly about the condition and impact of the entertainment media; about the fact that television and movies are not requirements or necessities for survival, and then decide what the reasonable response for a disciple of Christ would be.

The top television show in January '05 for kids ages 9-12 was Desperate Housewives. In the first season alone of Desperate Housewives, viewers were treated to an adult relationship with a minor, a drug dependency, a naked nanny, a suicide, a hit and run without any consequences, and images of strangulation. Teen characters are shown drinking, having sex with adults, taking drugs and deceiving their parents (Pavao). The message from Wisteria Lane begs an honest examination from God's people

First of all, is this neighborhood typical of your neighborhood? Of course not. While sin exists in your neighborhood, the depravity contained in a 60 minute episode of Desperate Housewives will not be occurring in your neighborhood in an entire year. (If it could happen in your neighborhood, you need to move...yesterday!) The devil would like to place somewhere in your subconscious that Wisteria Lane is really out there; that the mega-doses of sex, violence, and every-other-word profanity are somewhat typical of modern society. He loves for the workplace/schoolroom discussion the following morning to be laced with the titillating and lurid details of the episode and of what might happen next week. He wants us to think about the sexual images later and hear the dialogue replaying in our minds a few times when we go to bed that night and maybe the next day. He wants us to slowly become anesthetized to the shock of depravity and slowly become conditioned to accept it as typical of the world in which we live.

Then, when I face a temptation to engage in a racy conversation with someone other than my husband, or when some guy at the office shows me a little flirtatious attention, it won't be appalling at all to me. It will seem to be very innocent.... After all, it's really so benign when I think about it in the context of what's going on...out there. The sexual conversations that should vex our souls, as women of God, the gutter words that should wound our spirits... these dialogues no longer seem appalling at all. They are minor league compared with the images and dialogues to which we've become accustomed via that highly addictive screen in our own living rooms. Simply put, television today is conducive to adultery in your neighborhood.

Statistics are not the end-all, tell-all indicators about the anesthetization techniques the devil is using to promote the breakdown of family in our society. But they do give us somewhat of a baseline idea of his massive media takeover in our society and I pray that they will help God's people to recognize His manipulation of society through the entertainment media. Consider the following:

- Young people in the 90th percentile of television viewing have twice the predicted probability of initiating sexual intercourse than kids in the 10th percentile of television viewing (Berry, Collins, Elliott, Hunter, Kanouse, Kunkel and Miu).

- Sexual content is present in 70% of all programming. Programs with sexual content average 5 scenes per hour. Talk about sex is more frequent (61%) vs. overt images (32%) (Moraes).

- In a study performed by the Kaiser Foundation of 1000 shows in 2005, 4000 scenes had sexual content. This was twice as many scenes as was found in a 1998 study (Moraes).

- When thinking about healthy sexual choices, STDs and contraceptives, young people are almost as likely to get their information from television (60%) as they are to obtain it from a health care professional (62%) (Parent's Television Council).

- Kids spend more time watching TV than in any other activity except sleep (Parent's Television Council).

You may be thinking, "So what does television's impact on kids in America have to do with the vulnerability of my marriage? This seems like a leap to me."

It has much to do with the breakdown of family and the prevalence of adultery in our society. For three decades we've been serving up sexual fare to large numbers of America's children on a daily basis. The children of thirty years ago are now adults. They're the parents in your PTA. They're the coworkers in your office. They are even the church members on your pew. They are the desensitized adults, who are unable, without great effort, to be appalled, disgusted, shocked, or saddened when homes are broken around them because of unfaithfulness. They have been carrying images of illicit sex filed away at early ages for all of their adult lives. They have been replaying sexual conversations that were placed in their little minds far before they were able to process the moral implications of them. In many instances, guilt haunted and distorted their young hearts because of early exposure to sexual content. But they grew up under the steady manipulating influence of the devil, who wanted them to enter adulthood without any moral abhorrence of fornication and adultery. And in many cases, the devil was successful. This is, in large part, the reason my friend Patti recently commented, "I just cannot believe so many of the married people who work with me are very casual about going somewhere to have sex with a coworker during lunch hour. They know that we all know it's going on, but everybody is just so non-chalant about the whole thing anymore."

And about the movies...

What if I said to you, "There's a great looking guy who lives over in the projects. We can see through his back window from the alley between Second and Third Streets. He gets home from work at 6:30 and hops in the shower at about 7 pm. He's out at 7:05 and you get to see him come out of the bathroom in just his under-wear. It's really a pretty neat show. There are no curtains on the backside of his apartment since there are lots of trees back there. He lounges around till his girlfriend comes in and she gets undressed, too. Her shower time is around 8. Then she gets out (you get to see her naked from the waist up) and then she gives him a massage before they go to bed..."? Well, what if I said that to you?

You would obviously say, "I'm pretty sure Cindy Colley has lost her mind! Who does she think I am?...some sort of pervert?!" You would let me know in no uncertain terms that you're not about to engage in ridiculous behavior like I just described, and I hope you would be quick to go to the elders of my congregation and ask them to intervene in my life to help me with a serious sin problem.

But what if I ask you to over to the house to watch the latest

PG13 blockbuster movie with a bunch of friends? It's the movie that you've already seen at the theater and it was the top grossing movie of the year. The story line was riveting and it won three major awards. It did have a couple of scenes with partial nudity and implied approved illicit sex and a few "words", but it'll be a lot of fun to see it again. Well, if you're like most "Christians" today, your shock-o-meter just went down several degrees. This sort of invitation is not nearly so perverted as the former. You might have a pang of guilt as you think about whether or not Christ would accept such an invitation. You may realize it wouldn't be smart to take your teens with you. And some Christians I know would politely decline the invitation. But hardly anyone I know would use the word "perverted" in describing this invitation. And it would be rare indeed for an eldership to intervene in an attempt to keep members from viewing such a movie (though I'm deeply thankful to know a few who show such compassion and concern).

Is there really a difference? Is it a substantial difference? Do you see how the devil has successfully battered our purity, destroyed our consistency and dulled our moral senses?
It is past time for us to awake out of sleep and stop the hypocrisy of such fellowship with the unfruitful works of darkness because the days are evil (Ephesians 5:11-16)!

So what do we do about entertainment?

First of all, we repent. We just change our minds about entertainment. Decisions about the remote in your hand will be easy once you've adjusted your mentality about entertainment in general. Stop thinking "We need to stop at the video store and find something to watch," or "Let's see….It's Thursday. What's on tonight?" Start thinking "Entertainment is entirely optional and I am in control of both whether or not I am entertained *and* what forms of entertainment I choose. I will choose only forms of entertainment that bring glory to God in my life." You will find that once you understand that entertainment is not a necessity but is entirely optional, your life will be richer. Your marriage will benefit and you will soon become appalled at what you once allowed to come into your home and heart via the media. You will also become more creative and diverse as a couple once you explore other ways to spend time together. You will get to know each other more intimately.

Then...

- Determine that if you are watching television and a show contains cursing, the use of God's name in vain, gutter language, jokes about sex, or sexual content, you will immediately turn the TV off or change the channel. Plan to switch to the weather channel or the cooking channel when the commercials come on, because they are often very offensive to God's people.

- Even with the above rules in place, determine with your spouse a conservative daily television limit. This will help increase the interpersonal communication time between the two of you and with your children. Even if programming is clean, excessive amounts of television are unhealthy to relationships.

- Before watching a movie at home or at the theater (particularly if the movie was produced after 1959), visit www.screenit.com and get the lowdown on what objectionable material the movie contains.

- Purchase and install a device that mutes bad language (TV Guardian or a similar product). Remember, though, that this device only filters audio content. The visual images are still your responsibility. Thus the device is only helpful in viewing programming that is visually pure.

- Ask yourself "Would I feel comfortable watching this movie with Jesus Christ?" Then remember that, if you watch it at all, you will be watching with Jesus Christ, your omnipresent Lord.

- Give yourself another test. Ask "Would I want to be watching this movie when the Lord returns to claim His own?"

- When you decline (because of convictions) to watch movies with friends, always boldly (and kindly) state your reason for declining. This will help you avoid the same temptation recurring. It will also be a great start for more conversation about the Lord with your non-Christian friends.

• If thy television offend thee, cut it off (Matthew 5:30). Households with no television at all can function well. If you find that screen to be tempting, consuming, noisy and frustrating, get rid of the problem! In our house, we do have a television set. We do not have cable or a satellite dish and we do not pick up local stations well. So our television is used primarily for occasional movie nights. We love to sit down and watch an old movie together or an episode of "The Andy Griffith Show". But we also like table tennis, long neighborhood walks, board games, bowling, bookstore jaunts and antiquing together. Entertainment is optional. Entertainment is also more than what's on the screen.

Making these decisions together in your marriage will go a long way in making your home a haven for His glory. But you will also discover that adultery, fornication, provocative clothing and lewd talk will become more and more shocking to you in the outside arenas of your daily life. You will regain your shamefacedness or ability to blush (I Tim. 2:9). Your world will become less conducive to sexual temptation and adultery.

"Feel Good" Counseling

Perhaps the most blatant promotion of adultery and its ensuing tragedies in our society is the voice of "professionals"; social workers, psychology professors and counselors who have gone so far as to tout the "benefits" adultery can afford your marriage. "Healthy adultery" is acclaimed as the spice that draws married people closer together and invigorates the sexual relationship between spouses. Less outrageous, but more common (and more dangerous) are the marriage counselors and therapists who view divorce as a reasonable and often preferable option when marriages have problems of all sorts. Of course, when marriages end in divorce for reasons other than fornication, the probability of adultery occurring at some point down the road is great (Matthew 19:9). Several "Christian" women I've known have tragically relinquished their homes and children, fought bitter courtroom battles, wreaked havoc in the lives of the innocent, and ended up in adulterous relationships…all at the counsel of greedy lawyers and modern "therapists" who don't have God's will about marriage anywhere on the radar. I know these people. I know their children.

I watch those young lives struggling to find some semblance of normalcy and decency again. The innocent worlds of these children have been bombarded by adult sin and selfishness and they will never fully recover.

Will you please make a decision now? If and when you find your marriage in need of counsel and repair, will you determine to seek that counsel early? Will you seek help before the problems escalate into situations that seem insurmountable? Most importantly, will you seek counsel of someone who has great respect for the Bible and its principles of truth for marriage?

It may be the case that you can scarcely find a professional Christian counselor in your area; one who really believes and espouses the truths of God's word. It is better to seek the advice of wise and faithful Christians than to follow those who may be well educated in fields of psychology and social work, but who are not committed to Biblical truth. Studies have actually shown that lay counselors (those who are uncertified or untrained) actually can be as effective as those who have been trained. Lay counselors often appear to have a better ability to :

- Enter into the milieu of the distressed.
- Establish peer like relationships with those being helped.
- Take an active part in the client's life situation.
- Empathize more effectively with the client's style of life.
- Teach the client with the client's own frame of reference (Carkhuff).

The key factor in effective counseling is a genuine interest in helping; and often the faithful Christian friend is much more empathetic and interested than someone who may be socially and spiritually disconnected from the one seeking help. Truly godly elders, faithful evangelists and, perhaps most often, godly older women who meet the qualifications listed in Titus 2:3 are excellent starting points when seeking counsel. Often these people can find the resources you need even if they are unqualified to provide them. Pray as you seek counsel. If at all possible, seek counsel together, as a couple, and always stay in the Word as you seek resolution.

Remember, God hates divorce (Mal.2:16), but the devil loves it. He knows that divorce and adultery are close kinsmen and one is likely to precede or follow the other.

Think About It:

1. Have class members bring their own lists of verses from both Old and New Testaments that mention adultery with a specific consequence of the sin included in the verse. Discuss these warnings of inspiration and the seriousness of the sin.

2. Have a class member visit www.afa.org to present current information about objectionable television content. Have him present this material to the class along with suggestions about what can be done to voice objections to those who control this medium.

3. Have all class members visit www.screenit.com. to become familiar with the navigation of this site.

4. Challenge all class members to go on a TV fast for the next three weeks. At the end of the TV-free period, have an open and frank discussion about whether and how this time was productive or challenging.

5. Research counseling options in your geographic area. Are there qualified Christians? If possible, make a list of those in whom the elders of your congregation would have confidence. Include those who may not have all of the professional credentials, but who are "wisdom-tested and approved". Make sure all couples have this list for personal use or for sharing with others.

6. Have couples bring their top five "Things to Do Together for *Phileo* Development" to class. Remember, *phileo* is friendship love and it goes a long way in adultery prevention. Share these lists.

A House that's Truly Clean

I'm not a clutter person...I put things away.
I constantly remind the kids..."It's easier that way."
"When every item has a place and every item's in it,
It really saves a lot of time and we need every minute!"

I'm also big on hygiene. "Be sure to brush and floss!"
Everyone has check ups, no matter what the cost.
Once the kids came home from school infested with head lice.
We quickly bought the remedy and did full treatments...twice.

The bed sheets are changed weekly. The floors are daily swept.
The vanities are shining and the bedrooms neatly kept.
When the baby had a virus, I scrubbed and disinfected.
For other kids were in the house and they must be protected!

No raw meat on the counter, no raw eggs in the cream.
No drinking after others or swapping helmets with your team.
I take the baby wipes for our booth at Burger King
And we wouldn't touch that toilet at the Y for anything!

But do I live a cluttered life in a more important way?
I mean, do I make sure there is time for God inside my day?
Do I save a place for him in conversation and in prayer?

When my children watch my schedule, are they impressed that he is there?

While I'm so concerned that they are clean, and getting good nutrition,
Am I feeding them the Bread of Life? What of the soul's condition?
I lose my sanity when they come home from school with lice.
But they turn on the TV and none of us think twice.

As all the world's pollutants nestle snugly in their heads,
The lies, the cursing and filth remains, when I tuck them in their beds.
I kiss their sparkling foreheads and their freshly shampooed tresses,
I am not the least concerned about those mental messes.

The startling contradictions they must be thinking through
The difference in what's said at home and what's taught in Sunday school
The things that made Mom mad today, the things she rushed to do
And maybe even sadder still...the things Mom didn't do.

We didn't learn my memory verse. Our Bible time we missed
We didn't check on Sister Smith, but she's still on our list.
In fact I can't remember if we even said a prayer.
Oh yeah, Coach said one on the field...at least we made it there!

Kids know the stuff you think is neat. They see what makes you tick.
They know when you missed Bible class, you really weren't that sick.
They see what makes you happiest. They wait for your applause.
They know when you are angry and they contemplate the cause.

And so they're off to sleep, their teeth are brushed and clothes laid out
And Mom has just a moment to see what Daddy's all about.
He's glad to finally have a rest... a client made him late
He hasn't had his dinner yet and, my, it's half past eight!

He asks about that virus...if Timmy's finally fit.
He asks about the practice...Did Johnny get a hit?
He talks about his business deal, the merger he controls.
He talks of money, men and might, but not about their souls.

He says, "Are the kids asleep yet? You might want to close their door."
I want to turn the TV up. Tonight's the final four!
He gets worked up at the referees, but when the game is done
He says, "Did you get my shirts starched? I think I'm down to one?"

Clean shirts, clean cars, A clean bill of health. It's just the way we live.

We never stop to think of the impression that we give.
Those tiny hearts tucked into bed can see right through the clean.
They see misplaced priorities. They know just what we mean.

So when I grab that Pine Sol to wipe up those greasy splatters.
I say a prayer that He will help me see what really matters.
To know that in the scheme of things, these messes are so small.
For if I've made a mess of living, I have lost it all.

I thank him for the blood that is the cleanser for my soul.
I pray for wisdom as I let His purpose take control.
It's on the One who washes white as snow that I must lean
If I ever hope to live inside a house that's truly clean!

Cindy Colley

Works cited:

Berry, Sandra H, MA; Collins, Rebecca L.PhD; Elliott, Marc, PhD; Hunter, Sarah B.,PhD; Kanouse, David E.,PhD; Kunkel, Dale, PhD; and Miu, Angela, MS, (2004) *Watching Sex on Television Predicts Adolescent Initiation of Sexual Behavior*, Pediatrics, Vol.114 No.3, (Sept), pp.e280-e289

Carkhuff, Robert (1969) Helping and Human Relations, Vol. 1, Holt, Rinehart and Winston.

Moraes, Lisa (2005), "Television More Oversexed than Ever, Study Finds, The Washington Post, November 10, p.C01

Parent's Television Council (no date)), [On-Line] URL: http//parentstv.org/PTC/facts/mediafacts,

Pavao, Kate, (2006), Common Sense Review, [On-Line] URL: http//commonsensemedia.org/tv-reviews/Desperate-Housewives.html.

U.S. Department of Labor (2007) Quick Stats 2006 [On-line] URL: http//www.dol.gov/wb/stats/main.htm

When Money Is The Matter

The issue of money in marriage at first seems simple. Two intelligent, mature, young adults join their hearts, their lives, and their worldly possessions. They work and make money according to their talents and opportunities, and that amount dictates their purchasing abilities. Simple.

But if you're married you know the matter is much more complicated than that. Add to the mix that one mate was reared very frugally and the other was raised to always spend a little above whatever he/she made, and there's an issue. Throw in some college credit card debts that are accruing interest at warp speed, and now there are problems. And what happens when all the discretionary income for two years is spent in one fell swoop when he ups and buys that fishing boat or she buys that Miata? Sometimes the problems come even when both partners are frugal. Sometimes a hospitalization eats up all the savings and leaves insurmountable debt. Sometimes an automobile is badly damaged, but not totaled. This is complicated. It's been our experience that finances are one of the major sources of stress and problems among couples, and it well deserves a chapter in this book.

Jesus, who loved us so much and who created our world, had much to say about money. There was the dramatic and sobering meeting with the rich young ruler (Mk. 10:21) and the disturbing parable about the rich man and Lazarus (Lk. 16:16-31). He taught of a rich fool who, upon being blessed by God with much money, entered a sort of house of mirrors—all he could think of was himself (Lk. 12:16-21). In Matthew 6:21 Jesus taught us a sound value system when He said, "For where your treasure is, there will your heart be also." Money is not all there is. What Jesus wants us to know is that ultimately what really matters is people, and their relationships to Him. When tempted of the devil, Jesus said, "It is written, Man shall not live by bread alone, but by every word that proceeds from the mouth of God" (Matt. 4:4). In Mark 8:36 our

Lord asked, "What is a man profited if he shall gain the whole world and lose his own soul?" Here we are in the beginning of the twenty-first century, and our homes are still wrestling with that question. People have forfeited family, health and life to have more money. They've sacrificed the more meaningful things to their own peril.

In marriage, arguments over money often come from our having different value systems. While my hobby and the expense which accompanies it seem perfectly reasonable to me, my wife's hobby may be completely different, and require expenses too. What happens when one mate spends so much on his interests that there isn't enough left for hers? Let's address seven issues.

The Most Important Advice: Credit Is Dangerous. Handle With Care!

Did Jesus condemn the use of credit? No, as a matter of fact He used the concept of borrowing and repaying in Matthew 25 in the parable of the talents when He spoke of the one talent man who made nothing with his master's investment. The master chided, "Then you ought to have invested my money with the bankers, and at my coming I should have received what was my own with interest" (ESV).

But credit is far too accessible in our day. It can be used for every conceivable expenditure. Our college-age children receive a pile of advertisements weekly from credit card companies trying to lure them into long term, high interest loans. The same applies to young couples. It can be very tempting.

Many couples in financial trouble started down this road very early in marriage. I wish every couple planning matrimony could envision the slippery slope of financial heartache and how it often happens:

Before wedding bells quit vibrating they were arranging for loans for cars, refrigerators, and honeymoons which they couldn't afford to own. Two years into the marriage they decided to consolidate their debts into one loan. This maneuver helped them survive the moment, but it only forestalled the inevitable. They didn't change their spending habits and continued to use credit as a means of handling unexpected emergencies and for acquiring unnecessary items. Soon their monthly payments became too heavy again, only this time the outstanding debt was far greater. This led to feelings of hopelessness and guilt. They argued and blamed each other for their troubles. Larry Burkett, president of Christian Financial Concepts, stated that 80% of couples seeking divorce state that the focus of their disagreements is money (Burkett).

Credit can be a good thing. In most cases buying a house is a better long term plan than renting, but for a young couple that almost always involves borrowing. There clearly are emergencies where credit is valuable. But woe to that couple who signs away its future earnings without really counting the cost.

An elder friend of mine in Georgia told me that his father often said, "You can't drink yourself sober; you can't lie yourself out of trouble; and you can't borrow yourself out of debt." Pretty smart man.

The importance of communicating with your spouse

Money is either the best area of communication in marriage or the worst. Even before the wedding day a couple must deal with questions: Who is going to balance the checkbook? Who will oversee the monthly payments? How often will we eat out? What kind of car will we drive and how will we pay for it? Will we have a credit card and for what will it be used?

If a husband and wife can't have meaningful discussions and reach agreement on these subjects they probably cannot talk about the other vital areas of their marriage either. That's why a budget is so important.

The importance of budgeting

This is not always a popular idea but many have had bad experiences with budgets because they have misunderstood the concept.

There are generally three reasons why couples have failed in this area:

1. Some mates think the budget is a weapon they can use to attack their husband's or wife's spending habits. As a result, it becomes a source of constant bickering and fighting.

2. There are those who establish an unrealistic budget that inevitably ends up in the trash.

3. Many families try to correct three years of bad spending habits in three months. They become disillusioned with the process because they couldn't succeed immediately.

Budgeting is nothing more than a plan for spending. It doesn't just limit expenditures, it defines them. It makes this simple statement: "We have a given amount of income, and this is what we're going to do with it." Both husband and wife must be mature enough to have this discipline, to communicate, and to agree.

Budgeting should be done on an annual basis. It isn't a one month plan, it is a year-long plan.

First, as a general rule, plan to set aside over 10% to give to the church. While the Old Testament speaks of tithing a tenth of all goods, (Deut.14:22), the New Testament sets the amount more ambiguously: "...as he has been prospered..." (I Cor. 16:2). Today we are under a new covenant which is far superior to the old. It seems only reasonable to me that our giving percentage should be no less than that required by an inferior covenant.

Second, Uncle Sam will get his percentage. Sometimes withheld from your check.

Third, put money aside—no matter how small the amount must be—into your savings/investments. Now let's look at the remaining amount and divide it into several categories with corresponding percentages. These are not necessarily the percentages I'm suggesting for you, but merely guidelines to get you started.

1. Housing--35% (property taxes, utilities, mortgage/rent, and repairs)
2. Food-- 22%
3. Automobile-- 16% (car loan if necessary, fuel, repairs)
4. Insurance-- 6% (life, health, medical)
5. Clothing-- 5%
6. Entertainment-- 8% (recreation, Vacations)
7. Miscellaneous 8%

Obviously, these categories will vary according to a particular couple's priorities, preferences, and circumstances, but this is a good place to start.

Some suggest that it's a good idea to take the discretionary income (which requires actual choices instead of the power bill or the car payment), such as miscellaneous, clothing, entertainment, and food, and convert that much of your pay check to cash, putting the budgeted amount into an envelope marked appropriately for that expenditure. There is a huge psychological advantage to actually looking at the money you are spending, and how much is actually left.

Should the Wife And Mother Enter the Workplace?

There is a chapter devoted to this subject in this book, so I won't repeat all the reasons I believe mothers with young children should be stay-at-home moms. However, looking at it from a credit standpoint, two incomes do not always help. Often it accelerates the dilemma. Monica generates greater income, which will give her and Brandon a greater ability to borrow, and if they aren't highly disciplined, this can lead to greater debt. A vicious cycle can occur because she will soon be *forced* to work in order

In Mark 8:36 our Lord asked, "What is a man profited if he shall gain the whole world and lose his own soul?" Here we are in the beginning of the twenty-first century, and our homes are still wrestling with that question.

to make payments on further inflated loans. That stress can really rob a marriage of its music.

I'm impressed with couples such as Rob and Mallory who vowed at the beginning of their marriage that she would come home when the babies were born. They decided she would work outside the home at first, but that they would save her after-contribution-and-taxes income to help out when they had the babies. They would not develop a lifestyle dependent on two incomes. Now they have two girls, and are living on what his income will provide while she is full-time mom to those blessed children. By the way, those girls care more about having their mother with them every day than they would care to live in a bigger house or ride in a nicer car.

When we think of unreasonable spending and credit use, we may first think of the wives. But it isn't always her. Often it's the husband. On impulse, a woman may buy a relatively small dollar item--a blouse or a blender. On the same impulse, her husband may buy a boat, car, or airplane. One financial counselor I read said, "As a general rule, women are far more careful with money than men. They tend to be more security oriented and have an inherent fear of debt. For this reason, we always stress the importance of communication and balance in a couple's relationship and attitudes about money. The husband and wife must agree on a budget. A cooperative plan. God meant for you to be one flesh.

If your wife is working outside the home and someone else is taking a big chunk out of her child-rearing blessing, sit down with her right away and put a pencil to this matter. How much money is she actually bringing in when you consider the transportation expense, the clothing expense, taxes, childcare expense, etc... Then ask, "What could we do without for these eighteen or so years while the children are with us so that their Mother can stay with them?" Many couples, when they are determined, find that it can be done.

The Importance of Investing

The first rule: What works for one couple doesn't work for another. So...

1. Invest in things that have real value; items that have physical material assets. Be wary of large expenditures on things quickly outdated or "used up."

2. If you expect to live in the same place for more than two years, the best investment you can make is a home. While the payments do include a lot of interest, they also include principle which is growing. Furthermore, history shows that houses typically appreciate in value over the years. Be careful to buy in a neighborhood that is holding its property values.

3. If you have maintenance skills, and a little time, another great investment is rental property. If you have a little extra money and want it to work for you, buy a rental home, fix it up, and rent it. The value of that house will likely grow as fast as any investment, and it has real value. Everyone has to live somewhere, and rent payments will often pay the house payment plus the maintenance expenses. Be sure to always hire a home inspector before such a purchase to protect yourself from unseen, major problems in a

house. Be sure to rent to people who have good references.

4. Stay in familiar territory. Never invest in something you don't understand. Some men I know who lost their shirts did so by believing in other men who claimed they had a huge money making plan that couldn't fail. It failed.

One advisor said, "I have rarely met a doctor who makes money outside of medicine. Most physicians make their money in medicine and then lose it in egg farms, ranches, and oil wells."

5. It isn't a bad idea to find a financial advisor you trust, an investment broker, to help you get on the right track when you are first married.

Who Should Do The Book Keeping?

The one who is best at that sort of thing. I don't believe it has to be the husband. But keep God's system in place either way. A husband is to love his wife as Christ loved the church, and a wife is to see that she respects her husband as leader of the home.

Communicate. Get a budget. See it work on paper and then hang with it.

The Insurance Issue

How much life insurance is necessary? Life insurance should be determined in an amount which will protect the family's standard of living. A wise husband will consider his young children's education in the event of his death. He will want his wife have a home that's paid for. He'll want to provide all living expenses for a reasonable amount of time. Life Insurance should be used only to provide for the family's needs, never as a source of profit. Don't make the mistake of using your policy as an investment tool, because these plans offer a very poor return on the investment, and typically only serve the insurance company. What you get may not even keep pace with inflation. I suggest term insurance. Theoretically, you make your largest investments elsewhere and when you grow older and the insurance premiums are too expensive, you drop the insurance and rely on the money the investments provide.

What about health, home, and automobile insurance? My best wisdom is to worry less about protecting yourself from minor mishaps and be sure you're protected against the catastrophic. Carry higher deductibles and keep enough money in an interest-bearing account to pay them when you need to make a claim. Low deductibles translate into higher premiums and that money is just spent. With higher deductibles and a bank account for protection in case of claim, you pay yourself instead of the company. Shop insurance carriers. And as in most everything, it is good to find a Christian in the business whom you can trust for advice.

While the finances in marriage are important, don't let this become the centerpiece of your home. Act responsibly. Make a plan that will work, then implement it, and go on with your well-disciplined life. Work at living simply; beneath your means.

Think about it:

1. What is the biggest struggle you face with reference to finances in your marriage? (Note: "need more money" isn't an acceptable answer.) Are you and your spouse in general agreement about how the money is spent? On what day will the two of you schedule to make a detailed budget for the following year, including your financial goals?

2. What is it worth for Mom to stay home with the kids?

3. Research and warn group members about current scams to avoid.

4. List some businesses in which Christians should never invest.

5. Is it important for good stewards to be sure the money they leave behind at death will go to good and not evil causes? How can this be done?

My Legacy

When the last line has been written
And my time on earth is through,
What will my friends remember
When they see my empty pew?

Will they say I've gone to glory
And declare with certainty?
Or wonder if his grace is vast
Enough for even me?

Will they say, "This church will miss
Her great example to our youth"?
Will they say I led them Heavenward
If they really tell the truth?

What of my home and family?
If I reach my present goals,
Will I leave behind a spotless house
Or blood-cleansed spotless souls?

My legacy for others…
Just what's on the bottom line?
If it's figured all in dollars
I'll leave every cent behind.

But if my kids' inheritance
is faith and Purity
Then they Are very rich! My
Legacy will follow me!

    Cindy Colley

Works Cited:

Burkett, Larry Christian Financial Concepts [On-line], URL:http://www.crown.org/About Us

CHAPTER THIRTEEN

Is This Adultery Too?

I've just gotten off the phone with a brother in Christ who is separated from his wife and living with his aged mother, hoping the problems can be worked out. He dropped by his home when his wife wasn't there yesterday and discovered Victoria's Secret lingerie in the clothes dryer—lingerie that, in his mind, clearly evidences that she is unfaithful to him. Both this husband and wife are miserable and eager for divorce on this sunny day.

A chapter on this subject may seem strange, but hardly unreasonable, for the same Bible from which we get the teaching of successful, musical marriage also includes various warnings about marriage. We naturally protect that which is valuable to us. So does God. I have witnessed some of the most bitter divorce proceedings imaginable. In Mark 8:36 our Lord asked, "What is a man profited if he shall gain the whole world and lose his own soul?" Here we are in the beginning of the twenty-first century, and our homes are still wrestling with that question. Such hatred between estranged husbands and wives often knows no boundaries—especially where children are involved. Divorce without children is little league. Some warring couples need to spend a time in different towns to cool off, but they never do because of the larger issue of joint custody. Seeing one another weekly with the strain of meshing schedules keeps wounds open, bleeding, and salted. I hate divorce.

I counseled a woman for several months last year, though I never saw her face. All our conversations were about the torment of an adulterous husband, her sweet children, her parents and parents-in-law, and navigating through the swampland of divorce. The other woman in his life was vicious, and on one or two occasions relished telling her the details of her exploits with her husband. Although her husband denied ever sleeping with this woman in the same bed he nightly shared with his wife, the adulteress assured her that they had met there. Want to see the real pain of divorce? Picture that little wife dragging that queen-sized mattress out on the lawn for the garbage man to pick up. She went directly to the mattress store and bought the most expensive mattress they offered and charged it to her husband's credit card.

I've seen husbands and wives who once loved each other enough to vow holy matrimony come to the place where they cared about nothing more in this world than hurting the other.

One of the ways we want to motivate you to build a great marriage is to help you hate divorce. Read the following passages slowly and carefully. You may need to read some of them several times to digest the details of what is being said.

Therefore a man shall leave his father and his mother and hold fast to his wife, and they shall become one flesh, (Gen. 2:24).

You shall not commit adultery, (Ex. 20:14).

He who finds a wife finds a good thing, And obtains favor from the Lord, "(Prov 18:22).

For the Lord God of Israel says That He hates divorce, For it covers one's garment with violence," Says the LORD of hosts. Therefore take heed to your spirit, That you do not deal treacherously (Mal. 2:16).

And I say to you, whoever divorces his wife, except for sexual immorality, and marries another, commits adultery; and whoever marries her who is divorced commits adultery, (Matt. 19:9).

But I say to you that whoever divorces his wife for any reason except sexual immorality causes her to commit adultery; and whoever marries a woman who is divorced commits adultery, (Matt. 5:32).

So He said to them, "Whoever divorces his wife and marries another commits adultery against her. And if a woman divorces her husband and marries another, she commits adultery, (Mk. 10:11-12).

For the woman who has a husband is bound by the law to *her* husband as long as he lives. But if the husband dies, she is released from the law of *her* husband. So then if, while *her* husband lives, she marries another man, she will be called an adulteress; but if *her* husband dies, she is free from that law, so that she is no adulteress, though she has married another man. (Romans 7: 2-3).

Marriage *is* honorable among all, and the bed undefiled; but fornicators and adulterers God will judge, (Heb. 13:4).

I've got to do all I can to avoid being the kind of person my spouse will want to divorce. Studying *Your Singing My Song* together is a great start. Would you make these vows right now with me? Or, if you prefer, use this list as a guide to get you started, and make your own list with your spouse.

1. I will reassure my spouse often of my love. I will never end a phone conversation without saying "I love you."

2. I will avoid saying hysterical things, and never "put my foot over the fence" (i.e., "I have half a mind to walk out that door and never come back...", or, "I know the strongest, meanest lawyer in town and..." or, "The only thing that will make me happy is divorcing you...").

3. I will avoid all pornography, and all friendships that soften my resolve against adultery.

4. I will practice the law of safety with members of the opposite sex. See page 113 for the law.

5. I will stay away from people and places that present a temptation of adultery to me.

6. I will help my spouse with his/her problems, and practice unselfishness.

7. I will be what God wants me to be in this marriage whether or

not I believe my spouse is doing the same.

8. I will not refuse to seek counseling when we have problems and my spouse asks it of me.

9. I will read my Bible, pray every day and encourage my spouse to do it with me.

10. I will avoid all alcohol.

11. I will never lie to my husband/wife.

12. I will avoid retaliation when hurtful things are said to me.

13. I will rise every morning determined to be a Christian with every atom of my being, including when I'm with my spouse and things aren't going well.

14. I will avoid taking work which requires me to be apart from my spouse for long periods unless I have no other choice.

15. I will genuinely compliment my husband or wife at least once each day. I will compliment him/her in front of others and never criticize him/her before others.

16. I will unselfishly give myself to fulfilling my spouses sexual needs.

17. I will TALK to and LISTEN to my spouse every day in eye-to-eye, meaningful conversation.

There is one time in the New Testament when God says about a sinful husband, "Let him go." It's in I Corinthians 7:15-16; a case in which a believing wife is married to an unbelieving husband who chooses to leave her because she is a Christian. His departure does not give her the right to remarry, but her love for him and determination to hold to her faith, even if he leaves her because of it, may convince him to join her in Christianity. Verse 16 makes it clear that this is the meaning of the passage:

"But if the unbeliever departs, let him depart; a brother or a sister is not under bondage in such *cases*. But God has called us to peace. For how do you know, O wife, whether you will save *your* husband? Or how do you know, O husband, whether you will save *your* wife?" (I Cor. 7:15-16).

There is one circumstance under which God will permit divorcing one's mate and remarrying a suitable candidate while still having God's approval. As Matthew 19:9 teaches, it is divorcing a mate for his/her adultery, and marrying another. Underscore that the divorcing must be "for sexual immorality".

God never *demands* that a person divorce his mate. Sometimes you'll see two couples who have virtually identical problems. One will divorce while the other sticks it out and makes their marriage work with prayer, counseling and dedication. Try, try, try to make it work. Divorce is to be feared and should only be pursued if there is no other way.

> *Divorce doesn't start in the courtroom with his and her lawyers. It usually starts with a small grievance or negligence which is allowed to grow to monstrous proportions.*

Think About it:

1. Divorce doesn't start in the courtroom with his and her lawyers. It usually starts with a small grievance or negligence which is allowed to grow to monstrous proportions. Are there "small" matters in your marriage you need to address, correct, and then bury forever so they won't be allowed to grow larger?

2. Is there any such thing as a divorce without sin being involved somewhere? Explain.

3. When is the right time for a couple having problems to seek outside advice/counseling?

4. List the most important credentials for a marriage counselor, in order of importance.

5. Why do you think so many churches are failing to teach the truth clearly stated in Matthew 19:9? Are there religious people today who are living in adultery and don't even know it?

6. Turn to _____. Can you reaffirm the commitment you made when beginning this study? If so, please verbally make this commitment to your spouse.

The Race

There's only one chance at the crown that awaits
Only one lifetime to strive.
Only one finish that counts in this world.
And only the time you're alive.
Only one manual, one trainer, one chance.
Just time between you and the goal.
Only one foe to disqualify you
But this enemy runs for your soul.
This race is for brave-hearted, die hard achievers
For buffeting, disciplined focused believers.
For those who can throw off the weights that would slow them
For those who have studied the rules and who know them
For those who lean heartily on practice and skills,
But also on faith and an undeterred will.
So run, undistracted. Run fast toward the goal.
Keep steady, breathe deeply, and run for your soul.
The world is now small in the distance diminished.
The crown soon you'll wear...You're approaching the finish!
The glory of this crown dies not with applause.
This glory's forever, for it's in the cross!

    Cindy Colley